WILLIAM CAMPBELL PRESTON as a young man. From the original miniature on ivory by an unknown artist, now in the possession of Mr. Preston Davie of New York City.

The Reminiscences of William C. Preston

Edited by

MINNIE CLARE YARBOROUGH, PH.D.
Assistant Professor of English in Hunter College of the City of New York

CHAPEL HILL
THE UNIVERSITY OF NORTH CAROLINA PRESS
1933

COPYRIGHT, 1933, BY
THE UNIVERSITY OF NORTH CAROLINA PRESS

ACKNOWLEDGMENTS

I AM INDEBTED to the authorities of the University of South Carolina for permission to transcribe and edit these Reminiscences. For the illustrations in the book I am under obligations to Mr. Preston Davie, the owner of the miniatures reproduced.

CONTENTS

	PAGE
INTRODUCTION	ix
THE REMINISCENCES OF WILLIAM C. PRESTON	1
NOTES	125
CHRONOLOGY OF PRESTON	134
INDEX	137

INTRODUCTION

THE FOLLOWING "short and simple notices" were "set down" by William C. Preston near the end of his life for his namesake, Preston Rion, and were in the possession of the Rion family from 1860, the year of the writer's death, until the beginning of the present century, when they were acquired by the University of South Carolina through the efforts of Professor Edwin L. Green.

It is to be regretted that these *Reminiscences*, now published for the first time, cover only twenty-three years of a long and active career. Had Preston lived to complete his narrative, which breaks off with an account of his Continental travels, he would have dwelt, we may be sure, upon his student days in Edinburgh and his visits to Abbotsford, where Scott welcomed him as a guest; his return to Virginia, his admission to the bar, and his subsequent legal triumphs; his political activities, including his rôle as an ardent Nullifier, in South Carolina, his adopted state; his election to the United States Senate and his relations with John C. Calhoun; and finally his retirement from political office and his acceptance three years later of the presidency of his Alma Mater.

Though fragmentary, Preston's *Reminiscences* are entertaining and informing. Historically they are of rare value, throwing interesting side-lights upon many phases of early nineteenth-century life and characterizing important political and literary figures of the period. Wealthy, well-born, and well educated, Preston moved in the most distinguished company of his day, and was on intimate terms, even in his youth, with many of his illustrious contemporaries at home and abroad. Allusions and references of unique significance are made frequently, as might be expected, by an author who had had the good fortune to be visited in infancy by George Washington, petted and spoiled in boyhood by Dolly Madison, and introduced in young manhood to notables in Europe, by the President of the United States and other dignitaries of the nation.

Preston, it should be stated, had no intention of publishing his reminiscences. Among several unpublished letters to Mrs. William Martin of Columbia, South Carolina, which are now in the Library of the University of South Carolina, is one written during the latter part of his life, in which he informs his correspondent that he is diverting himself by recording for young Preston Rion personal experiences that already fill many pages. Declaring that these recollections are not to be read until after the author's death, he goes on to deplore his dullness of style. "I have always been ashamed of my writing," he confesses. "What little talent I had was in the gift of the gab, as we say in Scotland."

Preston's claims to distinction, as he himself points out, rest upon oratorical rather than upon literary abilities. As a public speaker he had few rivals. So famed was he, indeed, for his persuasive eloquence in the law courts and in legislative halls that he was generally regarded by his hearers as the equal in popular oratory of his maternal uncle, Patrick Henry.

More gifted as a speaker than as a writer, Preston is not, however, as poor a stylist as he complains of being. His published addresses are cultivated in tone, and the less florid passages in them are decidedly pleasing. That he could write a straightforward and vivacious narrative is evidenced by the following pages.

For the sake of clearness, a few changes have been made in Preston's punctuation and paragraphing, and his erratic spelling has been corrected. No further liberties have been taken with the manuscript. Despite the difficulties presented by Preston's handwriting, an accurate transcription has fortunately been obtainable, only a few words proving undecipherable.

MINNIE CLARE YARBOROUGH

Hunter College of
the City of New York

FRANCIS SMITH PRESTON AND SARAH BUCHANAN PRESTON, parents of William Campbell. From the original miniatures on ivory painted in 1794 by James Peale, now in the possession of Mr. Preston Davie of New York City.

THE REMINISCENCES

OF

WILLIAM C. PRESTON

I CONCUR WITH you my dear Kitty[1] that when Preston grows up he should know something of the person he was named for; I therefore set down for him these short and simple notices.

I was born in Philadelphia on the 27th of Decem. 1794, the first child of my parents.[2] My father was at that time a member of Congress from Virginia and thus it happened that I was born in Philadelphia instead of Washington County, Virginia. It was a tradition in my family that I was the first born of a government official at the seat of government and Washington being an acquaintance of my father and mother came to see the new born citizen. I can hardly persuade myself that I do not remember the scene of the illustrious man bending over my cradle and blessing the child, so vividly was it painted by my mother on my infant mind in childhood. My father was a member of Congress and his father[3] a conspicuous Whig of the Revolution, being Col. of the County of Augusta and thus in command of the militia from the Blue Ridge to the Mississippi. He commanded a regiment at Guilford. My mother was the only surviving child of Gen. Wm. Campbell of King's Mountain. She was a large heiress and my father too had hereditary wealth. My maternal grandmother was a sister of Patrick Henry. Thus I was well born and my mother in my childhood did not fail to let me understand it. She was a lady of beautiful person, a strong mind and a lofty character. Accustomed in her youth to the circle to which Washington gave the tone, her manners retained always a certain stateliness, which with her majestic person and high manners, made her a very conspicuous figure. Her wealth and her *manière à due* in some sort segregated her family from the poorer and plainer community in which she lived, and thus in my earlier childhood my associates were almost entirely domestic. The child next to me in age was Eliza, now Mrs. Carrington,[4] a clever, grave and precocious child, always ahead of me in whatever we engaged.

Our letters were taught to us by an Irishman named Peter Byrnes, a weaver by trade who had come into my grandfather's family as far back as 1780, and had continued to teach letters to successive children of the family and lived to teach her letters to my daughter Sally,[5] in 1824. He had always been a member of the Preston family, died in it at the age of 82 and is buried in the family grave yard at Aspenvale, Washington County, amidst numbers of his pupils, he being the only one (except another) a stranger to the blood whose remains are buried there. He taught us to read in the Testament and to cipher as far as the rule of three, which was the extent of his curriculum. I learned with facility and was I suppose of good behaviour—at least the *Master*, as all called him, never complained of us, and in after life confirmed the favourable opinion he had conceived of William and Eliza. We never failed to love and cherish him.

The next step in my education was to be placed under the tuition of a Mr. Hercules Whaley, a private tutor brought into the family, a man of rare and curious accomplishments. My father picked him up in remote valleys of Lee County, where he accidentally met him apparently shrinking from exposure and seeking obscurity. My father struck with his conversation prevailed upon him to enter our family as a tutor. He continued with us for many years but there was always a mystery hanging about him. In the course of time we gradually learned that he was a native of New York, that he had been bred for the ministry, that he had become an actor and at length had joined Gen. Wayne's army as a dragoon. These circumstances gradually dropped or rather leaked out in the course of our intimate relations with him for several years. He never entered upon any distinct account of himself and having dropped a hint, would lead off in some other direction. He was found to be a capital Latin scholar, familiar with the Classics contained in that language, not ignorant of Greek, and speaking French pretty well. Besides he had eminent skill in music, sang and played upon the violin with wonderful execution, and read and recited poetry with exquisite power. In reading to me fine passages of poetry he would be seized with such enthusiasm as to rise from his seat, assume a theatrical attitude in the floor and acclaim it with dramatic intonations swept away with excitement. So too playing on the violin (which he did from any music at sight) he would become entirely rapt and elicit the most exquisite tones. I can hardly restrain myself from drawing a full portrait of this strange and mysterious man. He took charge of my entire training (and slept in the same room); we cut our own wood and made our own fires. Each of us had two horses, groomed by ourselves, we rose and walked and sat together and slept in the same room, so that my process of education was continually going on. The only thing which we had not in common was my taste for hunting. With this he had no sympathy. I had a passion for dogs and guns. On the wild mountains and in the lonely valleys about the Saltworks,[6] with a gun in my hand I passed many hours day and night, solitary and alone. In the shade of deep hollows or on the sunny summit of some lofty mountain I staid frequently all day.

Whaley and I read together most of the Latin classics and many of the English, for my father had a very good library. But my parents thought (mistakenly as I have since believed) that their boy ought to be sent to a public school, and so at 14 I was sent to what was called the Washington College at Lexington,[7] a college superintended by lazy and ignorant Presbyterian preachers, and filled with dirty boys of low manners and morals. In six months at this place I unlearned as much as it was possible for a boy of sprightly parts to unlearn in six months, when being affected with some slight hemorrhage of the lungs my anxious parents thought it necessary for me to be sent into a Southern latitude and Florida was fixed on.

Mounted on horseback with a negro servant to wait on and to take charge of me, I proceeded on my lonely journey. Columbia lay in my way. There I put up at a tavern situated on the spot now occupied by the high sounding Congaree house—then bearing the most characteristic appellation of Goat-hall. There I met with several young men, Charleston boys who had come up to join the South Carolina College.[8] These youngsters whose address and manners were very attractive very easily persuaded me that I was far enough South for my health and that the new and flourishing college which they were about to enter was a fit place to obtain an education. So after a night of anxious thought I acquiesced. I knew that my father's plan of education for me was that I should go thro' some Southern College, then to Yale or Princeton and complete my course in Europe. His notion, impressed upon me from my earliest days, was that I was to be a well educated man and then to study law as my life time profession. This was always his purpose and my own never deviated from it. I entered the Sophomore class, December 1809, being a few days under 15 years old, but looking several years older, so that no questions were asked as to my age. In College I took and maintained a good stand. The state of discipline nor the course of instruction at that time were much calculated to confer a high education. I graduated with distinction in 1812, having gone thro pretty much such acquaintances as I had made under Whaley. I had a considerable reputation for speaking[9] and that was the principal source of reputation at that time. Legaré[10] and McDuffie[11] were the most distinguished students of my day, and they maintained it thro' life. Indeed I think that in most instances the relative position of students in College has been continued afterwards. When I was graduated I was not quite 18 years old.

Upon leaving college my father called me to Richmond where the Legislature was then in session that I might see the leading men of my own state. The most notable persons whom I met with were Messrs. Leigh,[12] Upshur,[13] Stevenson,[14] Moses of Hanover,[15] West,[16] Wickham[17] and some others whose names have survived to this day. From Richmond he sent me on to Washington City where were assembled the members of the war congress, Clay,[18] Cheves,[19] Calhoun,[20] Lowndes,[21] Bibb[22] and the rest. I was thrown a good deal amongst these men. Being a kinsman of Mrs. Madison and my father having been a colleague and intimate friend of Mr. Madison, I was domesticated by them in the President's house and there met with whatever was curious or conspicuous in the City. I forbear to note my impressions of men and things as I saw them in Mr. Madison's household and at his table. I of course saw and heard a great deal. Mr. Madison treated me with a kindness beyond his usual wont and Mrs. Madison with cordiality and even affection. She called me her own boy. She had been present at my birth and had nursed me in my cradle. The most affectionate relations existed between us all her life. I had in after life an opportunity to show my good will in some business she had before Congress when I was a member, and for some sessions I occupied her house on President Square after she had retired to the country. The most brilliant man of society whom I met with during that first visit to Washington was Gen. Wilkinson,[23] a man of very elegant conversation, of manners tending to display and ostentation and even to my youthful eyes then betraying a certain lubricity of character.

Mr. Madison's manners were somewhat cold and stiff, taciturn in general society and preoccupied. After dinner, however, at which he usually took a liberal portion of wine, he became free and even facetious, telling with great archness many anecdotes, and sometimes of a character not infrequent in the conversation of those days but now, in the improvement of manners, happily excluded from good society. All the gentlemen of that generation had fallen into this sort of talk, a practice which was said to have come to us from the higher circles of England where a foulness of conversation had been propagated by Mr. Fox and his boon companions. When I remember now talk that in my youth I heard from the most illustrious men, the Pinckneys[24] of Charleston, Giles[25] of Virginia, Crawford[26] of Georgia and others of that standing, it is with the deepest disgust. The change has come on within my observation of society and is thorough. It is not only that it seems so in my advancing age, for in my youth, men of my present age, were addicted to habitual smut, and persons of the most dignified stations and most exemplary life. Of the men whom I have known familiarly, Calhoun was the only one whose conversation was uncontaminated by such impurity. His words and his conduct thro' life were alike exempt from stain. While the bottle circulated freely at Mr. Madison's table, susceptible to its influence he talked a good deal. He enquired of his brother-in-law, Mr. Cutts,[27] always a guest, the news of the day, the proceedings of Congress, the audits, and seemed specially interested to know what Chief-Justice Marshall said and did. When Coles,[28] Cutts, Payne,[29] Todd,[30] and myself left the table Mr. Madison generally took a long nap in his chair, for I frequently found him there upon my return from an evening party whither it was my practice to go with Miss Mayo, afterwards Mrs. Gen. Scott,[31] and Miss Sally Coles, afterwards Mrs. Stevenson, young ladies like myself members of the household. On our return Mr. Madison would rouse himself and go into his study, for many hours, and he would be at his desk by candlelight in the morning. Mrs. Madison would frequently remonstrate against these consuming labours, but he declared that the pressure of the war business allowed him no alternative.

As to Mrs. Madison, the lofty and noble courtesy of her social life, was not less inborn and engrafted in her nature than the undeviating good temper and amity of her private life. Admirable and exquisite in both departments, [she was] a fit wife for a President, adorning the high circle over which it was her lot to preside and sweetening and soothing his private hours. It would be ungrateful in me now to mention her name without an expression of the love and admiration I have for her memory. Mr. Madison's toils and vexations, even at that early period of my life struck me as being hardly repaid by the dignity of his high office. He was exceedingly harassed, and manifestly defective in that vigour of character demanded by the very embarrassing circumstances in which he was placed. He wanted a talent for affairs, was deficient in tact, and in persistence of purpose. The opposition he was experiencing from the *Federalist* was a source of daily annoyance and vexation to him, exciting him to petulance and querulousness. When his secretary Coles or Mr. Cutts would repeat to him a violent speech of some northern man or a short sarcasm of Randolph[32] he would say pettishly, "The damned rascal! I wonder how he would conduct the government. It is easy for them to make speeches." Amidst the perplexity of his public affairs he did not see clearly and therefore did not step firmly. Nor did he seem to have any fixed purpose or have line of thought to which he could rally. His judgment was not clear about the war or the mode of conducting it, nor had he about him friends whose pertinacity and firmness might supply his own defects in these qualities.

The three ladies of the family were very striking women, first Mrs. Madison, then Miss Mayo, brilliant rather than beautiful, full of tact and talent and good temper, then my kinsman Miss Sally Coles, fascinating, gay, and fashionable. I was old enough to be a sort of residuary gallant for them, but too young to be suspected of the possibility of being a technical admirer, of presentable person and manner, and an avowed pet of Mrs. Madison. The season was gay and I very fully participated in it.[33]

At the end of the winter I had got enough of this sort of life, and I was taken home to rusticate for a short time, thence the next winter, my father thinking that I should be quieted down in a law office for a while sent me to Richmond to be entered in Mr. Wirt's[34] office, that I might take one other step in the education he proposed for me. The winter was passed in a worse than stationary, it was a retrograde condition. The style of manners amongst the young Virginia gentlemen was that of riot and dissipation and I have always looked back to this period with shame and regret. It was time worse than lost. Our set in Richmond was occasionally put to shame by the transient presence of Wm. C. Rives,[35] or Frank Gillmer,[36] but very few of our habitués escaped a melancholy destiny in after life and I am persuaded that I escaped the ordinary fate by a constitutional incapacity for drinking, which is hereditary in my family. No Preston has ever been addicted to that fatal Virginia vice of drunkenness and thus I escaped. We lived fast, were much addicted to cards, and had an unceasing round of gaiety, in short were persons of "wit and pleasure about town," holding in utter scorn all sedate pursuits or grave occupations. We were roisterers and it is mournful to look back on what became of the members of that winter's society. My friend John Bernard, survived into reputable old age and Meade into one of eminent vertue and piety. With these two my friendship continued until their death, Bernard's last year and Mead's 8 or 10 years ago. As for the rest of our boon companions, they are luckily long since forgotten.

My father's purpose to have my education finished in Europe was never relinquished. He thought it fit, however, that previous to a visit to Europe I should become acquainted with my own country, to which end with a pair of horses and a servant, he sent me on a journey thro Tennessee, Kentucky, Indiana, Illinois, and Missouri. It was a ride on horseback of four thousand miles with but occasional and accidental companionship. The ride was solitary, thro forests and prairies. It gave occasion for much musing and reveries, not as I think unimportant circumstances in the education of a youth, while my body was hardened by the exercise and exposure and my mind habituated to self-dependence. In Kentucky I made acquaintance with all the principal families, most of whom were variously connected with my own. Portions of Kentucky as it came from the hands of nature are perfectly beautiful, the land apparently a rich alluvian, so that riding thro its magnificent forests of noble trees one has the feeling of being on a rich bottom near a large stream. The principal inhabitants being well born Virginians, retained much of their native and early characteristics, modified, however, by some touch of influence from their new and raw condition. I will not say that the modification was a defect, for that might be a matter of taste and opinion, but it was different from a staid and settled society. The Browns and the Breckenridges and the Howards had lost a portion of Virginia caste and assumed something of Kentucky esteem, an absence of reticence and a presence of presumptuousness. Amongst persons of my own age, who were native to the state, there was a self-dependence not to say self-assertion, and ostentatious suppression of the smaller courtesies of life and minute observances of convention, which was not pleasant. When emigration to a new country takes place even in masses, civilization is not transported or preserved. New physical circumstances induce new developments, and a fermentation of society must take place. An old state of society cannot be propagated in a new country. A certain loss of civilization is inevitable. Stranger and hardier qualities may be superinduced, but they supplant the gentler and more refined. In Indiana and Illinois, society had not begun to be organized. The widely separated colonies surrounded by a small enclosure half field and half patch indicated an incipient comfort, and the worn woman of the house in compliance with the demand of a hungry traveller would in a trice produce a savoury cake and fried chicken or a venison steak, and freely enter upon conversation, until the arrival of another guest would recall her to her usual routine. Let me not omit to add to the real luxuries of chicken and venison, the uniform presence of a capital cup of coffee, not infrequently however sweetened with maple sugar or with wild honey, adulterations not pleasant but tolerable. In the meantime the good man of the house was off some 20 miles for a turn of meal from a mill or more frequently in the prairie with his gun, to get his family supply in the shape of deer, prairie hen or wild turkeys, and no fear that he would return full handed. As to sleeping, the man and wife occupied a sort of truckle bed in a corner, and the hospitable floor presented in its whole extent but scanty room for the numerous guests. I travelled a little more luxuriously than others with a pack horse laden with a little bread, my clothes, several buffalo robes, which last spread on the floor gave me comfortable bedding on which a day's ride of 40, 50 or 60 miles supplied the place of other luxuries. One day I remember I rode 72 miles across the big prairie, completed the journey between a little before day light and sundown, arranged my camp (for that night I camped out) before dark and strolled into the edge of the prairie out of a skirt of woods on a stream which had been designated as my lodging place, and as I stepped into the prairie across a fallen tree there sprung off a deer that at that distance of 15 or 20 steps stopped, turned, and gazed at me with an enquiring rather than scared look. I think he had never seen a man before. I clapped my hands to arouse his instinctive dread and felt oppressed by the solitude and remoteness of my situation. My riding horses were exceedingly fine, and the pack pony, a tough Indian bred animal, of inexhaustible endurance. I did not nor did my horses seem to suffer much from this ride of 72 miles. Those under the saddle were fully protected against the prairie flies by netting, and the Indian pony's hard hide seemed protected, though occasionally as we passed a tall clump of grass he would dash into it and brush off the swarms that beset him. Late in the night as I slumbered on my buffalo robe I was aroused by the tread of horses approaching on the path I had followed. Three mounted men rode up to my camp fire and called, "Hallo, there traveller." I said, "The same to you, gentlemen." I saw by the fire light, as they rode closely up three well mounted men of a grave and decent aspect. They turned out to be three Methodist preachers going out to Sangamon, to see if they could not get up a camp meeting, and establish a church. They told me that they travelled by night instead of by day to avoid the cruel annoyance of the prairie flies. They got down. I shared my supply of jerked venison with them. They rubbed down and watered their horses, and after an hour of pleasant talk we had prayers and the gospel wayfarers proceeded on their pious pilgrimage.

Two days afterwards I rode into the old town of Kaskaskia on a pleasant evening just as the people were going from Vespers. Amongst the men, women and children my attention was attracted by the tall and stately figure of an Indian, entirely naked, wending along with the crowd. Upon inquiry I was told that he was the last of the Kaskaskia tribe, it having passed away under the usual influences of contact with the white population. The ride hence to St. Louis is along the American Bottom, a bottom from six to ten miles wide and more than 100 long, entirely level, purely alluvial, bounded on the east by low hills or rather bluffs of Illinois and on the west by the majestic Mississippi close upon whose banks the road generally runs. Opposite St. Louis I crossed the river, standing on a platform erected across two huge canoes of black walnut, which were impelled by paddles like those of a steam-boat, and were worked by hand. Steam was not then (1816) on the Mississippi.

St. Louis was literally overflowing with emigrants,

portion of that flood that rolled to the west in 1816. One small tavern was stuffed so full that the nominal guests slept in the piazzas and in hay lofts. Many went out of an evening to camp in the neighbouring prairie. Meeting a gentleman in the door of the tavern he was kind enough to say to me, "I can give you a corner in the room of my printing press until you can look about for better accommodations."

From this hospitable tho not comfortable retreat I was next day extricated by Gov. Clark, (Lewis and Clark) an old friend of my family. The kind gentleman who had given me a roof to sleep under, was Mr. Charles the publisher of a newspaper.

In the elegant quarters of Gov. Clark I was domesticated during my sojourn and found myself most delightfully situated. Besides all appliances of comfort and elegance, I enjoyed the society of that most benevolent and intelligent gentleman, a man of primitive and heroic character, made up of firmness and tenderness, perfectly familiar with everything belonging to the Western Country, having been for years an Indian fighter, then associated in the expedition to the mouth of Columbia, and now for some time governor of the territory of Missouri. His military and civil functions were well and wisely administered. His wide jurisdiction over the Indians extending to the Rocky mountains over a vast and numerous population was efficiently and graciously exercised.

While I was of his household I associated daily with Indian Chiefs and others who came on business and besides had the opportunity of being present at a grand

Indian Council held to establish a pacification and make a treaty with a vast congregation of Indian tribes—Mandoes, Miamis, Osages, Sacs and Foxes, with fragmentary delegations from all quarters. They were encamped round about the town in every direction, occasionally tho rarely drunk in the streets, for they held Gov. Clark whom they called the Old White Chief in great awe. The Gov. was of remarkably fair complexion with gray locks and light blue eyes, hence the epithet *White* Chief. On the day of the solemn diplomatic session the Governor's large council chamber was adorned with a profuse and almost gorgeous display of ornamented and painted buffalo robes, numerous strings of wampum, every variety of work of porcupine quills, skins, horns, claws, and bird skins, numerous and large Calumets, arms of all sorts, saddles, bridles, spears, powder horns, plumes, red blankets and flags. In the center of the hall was a large long table, at one end of which sat the governor with a sword lying before him, and a large pipe in his hand. He wore the military hat and the regimentals of the army. Occasionally a chief came in, had a little conversation thro the interpreter with the Governor, and then retired with a slow and solemn step. By and by came in a somewhat miscellaneous troop, a sort of rabble, who formed round the table. The Gov. lit a large pipe; taking a puff or two, he handed [it] to some of the older men, pipes were lighted for the rest and they were invited to smoke. This was a short ceremony, and they were dismissed with a few kind words and altho mixed with warnings seemed to be satisfactory. At length there was a long loud roll of the drum, and an agent marshalled in the delegation of the Sacs and Foxes. This consisted of eight Chiefs, at the head of which was a chief leading in the son of the late King, a youth of 16 years old. His uncle was regent and guardian to the boy. He and the boy took their places at the end of the table opposite the Governor, the other chiefs seated themselves quietly on either side of the table according to rule of precedence that I could perceive. As they came in the Governor uttered no word nor made any salutation. Regarding them with a fixed and stern countenance he half unsheathed his sword and said: "Well, what have you to say?" There was a sort of gruff groan from each, and the regent rising from his seat, with his left hand on the shoulder of the prince, said: "I am not the King—he is dead. I have brought this boy here to our great father, to show you our confidence. The boy is too young to speak in council—these braves and I will speak for him." There was a general grunt of approbation and he sat down. There was a long pause; the interpreter whispered that they expected a pipe to be lit, but the Governor was imperturbable. At length a chief past middle life, rolled up in a long buffalo robe, having a red feather in his hair and his face very much painted, rose and said, "White Chief, we have come down to have a friendly talk with you. There is no more war in our hearts—(a general grunt) We are poor and needy, cold and hungry. We want something to eat, and ammunition to hunt game or we shall starve next winter. We will behave like dutiful children and never again molest our white brethren." "Who are you, you rascal?" exclaimed the Governor interrupting him—"I think I know you, (a general groan)." "I am," said the speaker, "the first man who broke into the settlement on the breaking out of the last war. I killed and scalped two women and a child. Here are the scalps," (taking them out of his pouch), and then I came on down to Pond Fort, where I burnt the stone. Here is my war path," said he, unfolding his robe upon the interior of which was rudely painted in red a long road, with bloody hands splotched along it, and at the end a picture of a conflagration. "I began the war," said he, "I fought thro it, and was the last to consent to peace, but I have consented, and shall be the last to violate it. Small as I seem to you to be I am a great warrior, a very great man, most as great as you. I have taken a great many scalps, stolen a great many horses with bridles and saddles—but now we are beaten and I give up. I have come down to beg peace, and flints and powder that I may hunt deer and buffalo. I have come down as softly as the dew falls at night, but if you refuse these presents the next time I will come like the Missouri in flood. Our horses have trod so gently that not a spark has been struck. If you refuse these presents I will come down like a prairie on fire. I have rode along bare backed on a little skew-bald pony with a hickory with bridle, but the next time we will come like a herd of buffalo, when they rush." All this was delivered in an even tone of voice, pausing at each sentence for the interpreter, and using throughout much gesticulation. The Chieftains from time to time had uttered their grunt of approbation. Several of the braves spoke in succession with much less animation, with ample profusions of penitence for the past and deprecation of further resentment, but all urgently begging for presents of ammunition, food, and clothing. When they had finished they asked that a pipe might pass around. The Governor said, "*No*, you shall not have a whiff—you are rogues, liars, and murderers. (There was a general groan) Go home as you came. I have made a straight path for you, swept it clean,—representing it on the table with the end of his sword—Don't turn on either side to the right or left; if you do my children shall whip you back. So go." They retired with a sorrowful aspect. The Governor sent the Interpreter to recall the Vice-King and the boy prince. They came in and the Governor handing them pipes, said to them, "You have done very wrong to bring that rascal with you on a peace visit. Take this rope to him and tell him that if I ever catch him in my country again I will hang him with such an one. Take these flints and this powder—take your people home and when they get there I will have some things given to them. Instruct this youth to be well behaved and to keep friends with the white men, and I will see that he is cared for."

The Chief who was closely enveloped up to the chin in his buffalo robe and wore no paint (being in mourning) or other ornament except a peacock's feather in his hat, rose to deliver a farewell address to the Governor. I have rarely beheld a more graceful or elegant speaker. He acknowledged the misconduct of his tribe but extenuated their conduct by setting forth the grievances and oppressions to which the White man had subjected it, and especially he complained that the Whites had associated themselves with the rascally and cowardly Osages, "each one of which big Indians is such a coward that tho he is as big as two men one of my braves can whip three of them." Growing excited in the progress of his speech, he threw the robe from his shoulders and it hung upon the leathern belt round his waist, leaving his whole bust naked except broad silver bands on each wrist and above each elbow making a fine contrast with his rich bronze skin. His gesture was free and graceful, dignified and deliberate, and when he spoke of the recent death of his brother and of the orphanage of the boy upon whose head he tenderly laid his hand, there was a pathos in the tone of his voice and his manner which one would have understood even without the very appropriate and pregnant words which the Interpreter rendered at the end of each sentence. I remembered these speeches for many years and often repeated them to my friends. In general the gestures and personal carriage especially the walk or running of the Indian is very ungraceful, but the whole bearing of this Vice-King was beautiful and majestic. There were several thousand Indians in and about St. Louis with great feasting and frolicking, and such was the influence had by Gov. Clark that there was no instance of violence, tho a good deal of drunkenness.

After a most pleasant sojourn of several weeks, I resumed my journey through Indiana and Missouri, passing Vincennes to Cincinnati—thence to Chillicothe, thence down to the Ohio at Point Pleasant, thence I traversed the wildest and most rugged region of Virginia to my home, having my horses tho wearied in good plight, upon which my father complimented me. I had rode about four thousand miles, had been on horseback nearly five months and had seen something of the New States and of the far West. "Spend the winter," said my father to me, "as diligently reading as you have the summer riding and in the spring you will be fit to go to Europe."

When the spring came preparations were in progress for my trip. Letters of introduction were procured from Mr. Jefferson and in February I went to Washington, Congress being in session, to procure others, for my father evidently thought that good letters were of great value to a young traveller in a foreign land. He therefore procured as many as he could get. Those which turned out of most value to me were some from the Abbè Corvea, the Portugese Minister, a scholar and man of science with something of a European reputation. I was in the city at the inauguration of Mr. Monroe[87] and from long and intimate friendship between him and my family he was very kind in furnishing me [letters]. Of special importance to me was one written on the day of the inauguration to his friend Lord Holland announcing that fact to his Lordship and commending me as a friend who was seated by him at the table as he wrote, written in terms doubtless prompted by the excitement of the moment. He also gave me a general letter to all officers of the Government in foreign Countries. Besides these and a few such like, I got piles of letters to English merchants and men of business, directed after this fashion. "To Messrs A. B. C. and Sons, Fenchurch Street, London, to Messrs Widow A. B., and Brown, 178 Strand, London, etc. etc." which while in England having delivered a half a dozen of them and finding each one exactly of the same stamp, I burnt the whole pile and thus saved the expense of coach hire by dining at a coffee house.

Before sailing I spent 10 days in New York at the boarding house of Mrs. Bradish,[38] where there was as stately a ceremonial as I ever afterwards found in the palace of a nobleman. There were several of the men of wit and literature about town, Mr. Bradish,[39] Mr. Verplanck,[40] an editor or two. The tone was snarling and pretentious and when I enquired as to certain gentlemen to whom I had letters of introduction, there was a turning up of noses at them. I dined at Dr. Hosack's,[41] with Dr. Francis,[42] Dr. McNeven,[43] Dr. Mitchell[44] and others who in turn turned up their noses, at the light and frivolous contributions to the press. I dined with Prime Ward and Co. at Mr. Prime's[45] elegant establishment and here the rich men of business turned up their noses at the musty philosophers and would be wits. The entertainment was somewhat too elegant, but upon the whole they were pleasanter people and more men of society than those of the other cliques. Each it seemed to me was unfortunately repellent of the other circle. Let me mention with gratitude that each set gave me letters of introduction to England. I suppose they found something attractive or amusing in the raw young stranger from the South, mixed with a certain consciousness of being well born and entitled to position. I did not feel that I was like to be an object of slight, and do not remember except on one occasion which I shall hereafter mention that I felt that I would assert my right to be considered.

In May I sailed for England, in the good Quaker ship Amité one of [a] line owned by a company of Quakers, Lawrence and Co. The passengers were numerous, of all countries and entirely uninteresting. I don't believe I remember the name of one. A run of 30 days brought us to the coast of Ireland, off the Cove of Cork. On a bright fair summer morning we hastened to the deck to rejoice our eyes with the sight of land, and in a few minutes came alongside a fishing smack to sell fish. While the Captain was bargaining for them, I was ready to get aboard, had engaged the fisherman to carry me up to Cork, and taking what coin I had or could borrow, with a single trunk of clothes, and leaving my letters and every thing aboard, I determined to run thro Ireland, and meet my companions of the voyage at Liverpool.

There is hardly in the world anything more beautiful than the Cove of Cork, with its sloping banks of grass down to the water's edge. To my sea wearied eyes, it affected me with rapturous delight. One of the boatmen had lost an eye, another a leg, and all the four were as rough and squalid a set as I had ever seen, but they were animated by a certain quizzical good temper, which seemed amused at my raptures and delight and the eager questions I put about every object seen on the shore as we passed. Seeing a little boat house with a painted boat lying near it, I asked to be put ashore that I might look at it. The man at the helm said, "Our time, your honour, is valuable to us." "Then," said I, "here's half a crown. Give me that much of it." "That's an hour," said he, "and you may have as many as you please at that price." So we drove up beside the little wharf and stepping on the earth, I reeled off, nearly falling, the boatmen exclaiming, "Take care of your sea legs." I threw myself upon the rich sod and wallowed on it with delight. Such a sod. Soft, thick, and of pure emerald green, I had never seen any thing like it, nor as I think since. As we neared the City I asked where they would recommend me to put up. They answered—"The Captain told us to take you to the 'Duke's Arms' and get a receipt for me." So to the Duke's Arms I went, and as I handed a couple of crown pieces, One Leg said, touching his hat, "It is your honour's generosity, not our charge. God bless you. I wish I was in your free country with you." The hotel was a capital one opposite a large square. As I sat in my chair and all night as I lay in bed I was tossing uncomfortably, and hardly recovered upon a capital breakfast. One is sensible of the comforts of being ashore who has been weeks afloat. No possible appliances can render being on ship other than uncomfortable. The mode of existence is unnatural.

From my windows the next morning, looking upon the public square I found it covered with a dense crowd of sturdy and stalwart peasants, with a patient but surly air. They filled the enclosure of the square like cattle in a pound. Upon going down to ascertain the meaning of the assembly I found they were labouring countrymen from the surrounding neighborhood who had come in to see if they could get employment in the then approaching harvest. Some were provided with scythes and others with other implements of labour. They stood there all day. Some seemed to be provided with a scant allowance of food, many apparently without any. I went in amongst them. Several were employed by gentlemen, who came and inspected them and took such as they fancied. There was, as I could perceive, no bargaining. The gentleman said, "I will take you and you." I suppose the hire was fixed and known. Those selected stepped forward with an air of alacrity and followed the employer. Many of them said they were hungry, and all looked so. A cart of bread passed by. I told one with whom I was talking to buy it for me and divide the bread amongst them. He stepped forward and said, "What will you take for the bread in the cart?" The driver hesitated to answer, and my man perceiving it, pointed to me. Upon seeing me the driver said, "a guinea." My man said, "I will give you 15 shillings which is more than you and your bread, and scrawny cattle are all worth." "The bread is yours," said the driver. "I would not take it from you, you scalper, but from the gentleman," bowing to me. So the bread was distributed, and my man said, "I have saved your honour six shillings which I will buy for you in beer, from yonder shop as sure, your honour, the bread is very dry." The beer was brought in three tin buckets, with a couple of tankards. As he took the first draught he said, "Here's to your honour, and to your noble Country of America. Long life to you." All round the square were crowds of women and children, most importunate beggars. I was glad to retreat when my last copper was exhausted.

Late in the evening I got into the Clonmel coach, on my way for Dublin. It was a superb vehicle drawn by four spanking horses. Besides the coachman, a great fat man rolled up in a drab great coat, there was on the rear of the coach an equally fat man in a bright red wescoat with metal buttons; he I understood was the guard. He had two large pistols in his belt and a carbine lying on the coach before him. The lamps were lighted and as we left the City a file of dragoons rode up on either side. Thus attended, we proceeded at a moderate pace of about five miles an hour. The closing in of dusk gave me an opportunity of reflecting upon the novelty of my situation. From my fellow passengers I learned that the reason of the military escort, was for protection through a country of extreme disorganization and turbulence which had been recently put under the ban of the insurrection law, called the Peel Act. Curious to see a population in this condition of turbulence and enforced suppression, I left the coach at Clonmel that I might in the first place visit Cahir Castle and Cahir Cottage in the neighborhood and then traverse leisurely the disaffected territory. Cahir Cottage is an exquisite exhibition of taste and luxury, built on the summit of a rock, round which is made earth for shrubbery and gardens, the rock is perforated through and through by galleries and grottos—and the gem of a house finished and furnished with whatever the wantonness of wealth could buy. The neighborhood was in a state of starvation and necessarily so demoralized that there were daily shooting and hanging. There were several gibbets from which bodies were dangling, one having as many as three. By the Peel Act, as I understand, a military police was stationed in the country with power to arrest and try summarily before a court-martial persons suspected of crime or misdemeanor, with power to shoot, hang or transport them. One of the provisions of the act was that a person found out of his prescribed bounds between Sun and Sun, without a satisfactory excuse should be transported. Cahir Castle was the first I saw of those large stone monuments of feudal times, which had always filled my imagination with wonder and romance. This specimen is a very fine one, a noble wreck in ruinous perfection. I never passed near one of these old monuments without turning aside to contemplate it. Passing thro the counties of Limerick and Tipperary, I often saw peasants flying from the approach of my carriage and when I visited a hut the man slipped out the back way and the surly woman would pretend not to understand English. An assurance that I was not a *Peeler*, but an American, generally restored confidence, which was confirmed when I gave a sixpence. The interior of the huts was of indescribable squalor, revolting and horrid—in one corner generally a pile of half rotted potatoes, at the door sill a mud hole, piles of filthy rags in the corners, children naked, and not one article of comfort or necessity. Thro such scenes I passed on to Tipperary and Limerick and then took my way to Dublin. My route lay thro a fine country, the lands were rich and highly cultivated, and the landscape beautiful. Beggary, starvation, crime, and punishment were on every side.

As I got into Dublin on an evening the drunken postilion had so exhausted his horses that at the head of the street they refused to go and when beating was obviously ineffectual I got out, upbraided him and refused to give him the customary fee, as by his misconduct he put me down in the street instead of taking me on to the hotel. We of course had a controversy, in which I was like to get the worse when there drove up two gentlemen in a jaunting car, who chid the ruffian with an air of authority, and offered me a seat in the car down to the Hibernian hotel. To my lavish expression of thanks they replied it was only what was due to a stranger, a gentleman, and that they were more than repaid by making the acquaintance of an American. That evening I went to the theatre and heard Braham[46] sing, "Scots wha hae with Wallace" and "Love's Young Dream." In Dublin I had no acquaintances, and no letters to make any as it had not been in the project of my route. After breakfast next morning as I was walking in a somewhat disconsolate mood thro the reading room, to my utter surprise and unbounded delight I met my friend and kinsman Mr. Edward Coles, who, as it turned out, was going on a secret mission from the President to the Czar of Russia to accommode some recent offence given to that court. [See note 28] Coles had letters of introduction and money, both of which I wanted, for the small quantity of coin I had brought from the ship had been drawn from me by the beggary and want along the road. My letters of credit were upon Liverpool. Coles and I in a jaunting car drove round to deliver his letter to Mr. Hamilton Rowan,[47] a name very familiar to me. He received us with the utmost possible politeness. He was a grave, good looking gentleman, just passing middle life. While I looked at him and talked with him I was all the while thinking of Curran's speech,[48] which at that time I knew entirely by heart. In the course of conversation I accidentally dropped an expression from that speech. He smiled and said, "I believe that you in America have heard of my name connected with those sad times of Ireland." He invited us to stay to dinner, but as we could not he said he would go round with us to Sir Charles Morgan's. To him or rather to Lady Morgan, formerly Miss Owenson, Coles had very special letters. So Mr. Rowan dismissed our hired car, and took us in his. I had never met a person who had written a book and I did not contemplate such an incident without emotion, and a lady author too. I had read in my childhood "The Wild Irish Girl" and thought of course that Lady Morgan was *Glorvina*.[49] Having been seated a few moments in the drawing room, came running down somewhat heavily a fat red-cheeked, cock-eyed lady, any thing in the world but the airy Glorvina of my imagination. Seeing three gentlemen she exclaimed, "Which is Mr. Coles?" He was presented and saluted brusquely and warmly, she talking all the while. I was then presented. She said, "You naughty old Mr. Rowan. I *will* call you old, you have not been to see me for an age, but I forgive you as you have brought a propitiation in these Americans," and thus she ran on, pausing for no reply. At length turning to me, she said, "You, too, a *Yankee?*" "No, your ladyship, I am a Virginian." "Aye," said she, "a proud Virginian. To us you are all Yankees, rascals who cheat the whole world. Even I have suffered from you, for you have cheated me out of my copy-rights. You have all read my works and have paid me nothing for them." "I pray your ladyship my most hearty thanks, and I am not accessory to the theft of the book sellers. Indeed it is of that kind in which the law does not admit of accessories." "Hah," said she, "I am lawyer enough to know that in treason and petit larceny all are principals. You are a lawyer, I suppose." "No Madam, but a culprit confessing himself guilty of treason, participating in all your ladyship's Irish feelings, to which you have seduced very many of my country."[50] "Hah! well, but you are rogues all." The lady seemed kind, vain and somewhat coarse, which impressions of her were confirmed by a subsequent familiar acquaintance in Paris.

I went to the four courts. The outer room was a crowded scene of wigs and black gowns. The hall was filled with lawyers as I had seen the square with peasants, and their looks were hardly less eager and hungry. Mr. Rowan pointed out to me counsellor Philips[51] as a young man of promise and a year or two afterwards his name became celebrated as one who exaggerating the falsetto style of Irish eloquence made it ludicrous and monstrous. The genus of this mode of speaking, a sort of bombastic display, was found in Grattan and Curran, both of them without this and even with it, great orators. Indeed, one might detect it even in Burke, in whom with his great intellectual ardor, there was an absence of that passionateness which burns up forms of speech, and makes rhythmical utterance disappear in a molten flood of metal. Philips had the merit requiring doubtless some genius to extinguish this false taste by an inimitable parody and burlesque, which showed at once that it ought not to be imitated and was inimitable. High artists have imitated the Greek but the arabesque imitators are ludicrous.

When I got to the wharf to take the packet for Holyhead, a piteous spectacle was presented. It was a jam of poor and sturdy peasants, trying to get on board for going over to England, to get work in the harvest. The owner of the packet had put the passage at half price and at the instant that the bar was removed enough to cover the whole deck rushed on, many who were not able to pay and when notice being given that such should not be landed at Holyhead, many struggled back. As it was the crowd aboard was prodigious and squalid. The pay passengers bought all the bread in the vessel for their use, and I was drained of my money so as to leave barely enough for me to get to Liverpool on the outside of the coach. When I got there I had but two and sixpence in my pocket. It rained heavily and incessantly the whole way and before we got to the City I was seized with a chill which shook me with great violence. The Coachie seeing it, proposed at one of his drinking places that I should have a glass of hot negus, which may have been a wrong prescription but it gave me presence of mind to tell him that when we got to the City I desired to be driven to the King's Arms and that I was an American. This was a lucky communication for me, for a fever coming on I was somewhat delirious when we got to the King's Arms and lost all consciousness when I was carried into the house, nor had I the slightest recollection for some days. When my delirium passed off at length it was suddenly, and rising on my elbow in bed, I saw standing near me a rosy cheeked, tidy looking girl. Looking at her a moment, and endeavoring to recall my consciousness, I said, "Rosebud, who are you?" She dropped a little curtsey and said in a startled voice, "I am not Rosebud, your honour. My name is Betty," and she left the room. While I was trying to find out if I were not dreaming, the girl returned with a small gentleman dressed in black, [who] said to me in a kind tone: "The doctor said if the anodyne had its expected effect you would probably awake relieved. I hope it is so." "I do not know," said I. "I know nothing about it. Where am I?" He said, "I am your countryman, Washington Irving," and gave me to understand that being ill and delirious at the King's Arms, they had sent for the United States Consul, who, opening my trunk, found my letters one of which was an introduction to him from Mr. Jefferson,—he took possession of me and my effects, employed a Doctor and had me transferred to private lodgings, where he with Mr. Irving and Mr. Brown the banker had been in attendance on me. While we yet talked, Mr. Maury,[52] the venerable old gentleman, came in, having been sent for. He extended his arms over me, and said, "Thank God, young man, I hear you are recovered, but I must continue to have jurisdiction over you until you grow strong. For the present you must lie still until the Doctor gives permission." A day or two brought the permission. The excellent old gentleman took me to his own house where I was under the care of his family and had daily visits from Mr. Irving and other Countrymen. Old Mr. Maury, who had been appointed Consul by Washington, held the office with undivided approbation of all ranks and conditions of men, foreigners and countrymen, until under the ruthless administration of Gen. Jackson he was turned out to make room for some divider of the spoils. Not even the recklessness of Jackson or of his ferocious and unscrupulous followers could say aught of the old man, but that his services had been long and faithful, too faithful for those who would have official functions made subsidiary to party purposes, and too long for those who were impatient for their portion of the spoils. His conduct to me was fatherly,—and that it was so to all, every American who was ever in Liverpool bore testimony.

The tenderness and attention which I received from Mr. Irving were consistent with his kind and generous nature. I found him a man of grave, indeed a melancholy aspect, of very staid manners, his kindness rather the offspring of principle and cultivated taste than of emotion. There was an unfailing air of moderation about him, his dress was punctilious, his tone of talking, soft and firm, and in general over subdued, until a natural turn would occasionally run into humour, and laughable delineation of character or events. During my convalescence, which was somewhat tedious, our acquaintance ripened into some degree of intimacy and I freely disclosed to him my condition, my plans, and my purposes. He was eight years my senior,[53] had seen a good deal of society and had made for himself an honourable name. He was then eminently fit to exercise a large influence over me,—especially in restraining the exuberance of my national and natural temper. Of that characteristic of our country he had great dread and distaste. It was foreign to his peculiar idiosyncrasy—he called it whether in conduct or in conversation or in writing *Americanizing* and in himself pushed his opposition to this tendency to the extent almost of affectation. He had a great deal of the English reticence. With them it is, as it was not with him, a surly and ill mannered and unsympathyzing manner. It is a national character resulting from the false and foolish notion that true dignity is to be always on the watch for aggression and that *nihil admirari* is elegant and aristocratic. All emotion is vulgar and ardor horrible. Towards this Anglicism there was some little tendency in Irving—propriety, fitness, retention were what he admired. His great kindness to me made him sensible of my defects in these particulars, and he was free in his animadversions after we had become familiar. I vindicated myself upon the ground that they were nationalities, but he replied that they were wrong nationalities and ought to be suppressed in a gentleman,— that to suppress such things was one object of travel. Although in the warmth of such discussions Mr. Irving occasionally grew warm, and I did not seem to yield, yet he soon became cool and upon subsequent reflection I saw much truth in what he said. He was a good deal preoccupied in the first instance, by the disastrous condition of his pecuniary circumstances. In regard to which I learned from him that he had set out from America with ample means to meet the expenses of his European travel, which was projected for three years and as far as Italy and Greece. Upon getting to Liverpool his brother and brother-in-law thought that the provision he made was hardly ample enough and to make it so recommended that he should place his capital [with them] and become a partner in the then very prosperous firm, so that he would be entitled to draw for whatever he might desire. His name was therefore entered in the books as partner, and at the end of a few months the flourishing business was suddenly struck by a disastrous commercial revulsion, which amidst a general desolation, swept Irving's into utter bankruptcy. "I found myself," said Irving, "worth much less than nothing, and it was a relief to me to hear that my mother had died just before the crash. It involved the destruction of some other arrangements that my heart had been set upon."

Another subject somewhat connected with this was how he should turn his literary efforts into some profitable direction. Hitherto literature had been an amusement. He had written Salmagundi, Knickerbocker, and the sketch of the life of Thomas Campbell (Pleasures of Hope) prefixed to an American collection of his works. The sketch of Campbell had brought him in communication with the poet, and led to a pleasant correspondence, in the course of which Campbell had intimated an opinion of Irving's success before the British public if he would attempt some suitable work. Irving decided that literature was to be his profession and the means of support. He had taken lessons in drawing, and had a decided turn for the art. He sketched very well, even in the estimation of Washington Allston,[54] Leslie,[55] and Stewart Newton,[56] and it was perhaps some feeling of this kind that suggested to him the notion of his Sketch Book. He turned it in his mind—spoke a good deal to me about it—occasionally asked me when he gave an account of anything that touched him, how would that do in print. We went to the Athenaeum together and on our return he jotted down what he saw or what had struck him.[57]

He advised me not to go up to London to deliver my letters of introduction to the notables there until my European tour was in some measure finished and proposed that he, his brother Peter, and I should make a pedestrian excursion into Wales *en attendant*. We made frequent visits to Halton Castle at the village of Runcorn, on the Mersey some miles above Liverpool. It was the ruins of a grand old castle, frowning over a large extent of green pasture through which the Duke of Bridgewater's canal could be seen for miles like a silver thread. Round the base of the rock clustered the little village of Runcorn. At a short distance was seen the residence of Sir James Brook, I think the name was. Amidst the broken wall and on the rocks, was constructed a nice little English Inn, kept with the most exquisite neatness, adjoining was the Parish Church, and close by in one of the preserved rooms of the castle was an old library, founded some centuries ago by some member of the Cholmondeley family. The librarian was the parish priest. The books were antiquated, not often disturbed, they were mostly in Latin in a small quarto shape, strongly bound. Some of them had attached a small chain, so that one had to stand or to sit on a high stool to consult them (I think in some of his works Irving has drawn a picture of this library). There was a bowling green in the front court of the castle and in a corner, the residence of a keeper, who held the house and a rood or two of land by the tenure of holding the stirrup of Sir Charles' [Sir Charles is at variance with the former reference to Sir James] saddle when he rode up to church. The occupant at that time was a tall soldierly grey haired man with his sword, stirrups and spears over his mantel piece. He had been an English trooper in America in the war of the Revolution. His recollections of the country or the events of the war were very vague, but when he had drank a stoup of ale he would vaunt somewhat of how he had chased the rebels and he himself got caught. The massive ruins of the old castle reposing amidst ivy upon the summit of a perpendicular rock, with the wide prospect of champagne country around was as picturesque as could be conceived of. Of a Sunday the peasantry assembled to church, to drink ale and to play at Bowles. We could see from the battlement when Sir Charles with his groom mounted to ride to church, the castle bell sounding its loud tones down to the stately mansion.

The old soldier would take his station near the stone clock, watching the approach of the lord of the manor, and taking the bridle in one hand, held the stirrup with the other, at which moment the church bell tolled. The whole scene was entirely feudal. Sometimes of a Sunday evening when the game of Bowles became interesting the parson would join in it and occasionally—it must be admitted—he took somewhat more ale than became his cloth, but that liquor rarely prompts to those indecent exposures produced by our more alcoholic drinks, but on the contrary increased the gravity of his demeanour, and the effects of the liquor were perceptible only in his wide bowling. On such occasions the humour of Peter Irving became exquisite. He was an elder brother of Washington, was an old bachelor, an eccentric humourist, of a very grave aspect and full of fun. In the composition of Salmagundi [he contributed to] the poetical department, under the sobriquet of Peter Cockloft,[58] and he at the time I speak of continued to write poetry. When the fortunes of the family by the success of Washington grew better he was finally settled in a nice suite of rooms in Paris on [the] Rue [de] Rivoli within an easy walk of the Tuilleries garden, where he spent the residue of his days, living as I have heard, to a good old age.[59] I suppose he must have been ten years older than Washington.

At length the time came for our excursion into Wales. Our wardrobe consisted of two shirts made of linen cambric, compressible into so small a space that they with a pair of silk socks were put into the crown of our hats. It was arranged that our wardrobe and trunks should be sent by public conveyance from place to place. By the coach we went to Chester, that strange old town with the upper stories of the houses projecting over the side walks so as to make a perfect protection from the weather; hence we set out afoot for Wrexham, where I beheld with admiration an exquisite piece of sculpture by Roubillac,[60] a monument representing in relief an angel sounding a trumpet, a tomb stone breaking in two and a beautiful female figure rising through the aperture. It was the first piece of high art I had ever seen and its impression is vivid on my mind to this day.

Our progress from Wrexham to Llangollen, taught me that though mountain bred and accustomed all my life to hunting on foot I was inferior as a walker to the city-bred Irvings. My feet gave out, became swollen and painful and when we got to the high ridge over Llangollen, I was broken down, and compelled to take shelter in a substantial farm house. We were hospitably received. Ale and brown bread were handed to us, and falling into conversation our host upon being complimented upon the fine situation of his house overlooking the valley of Llangollen, and his household presenting an air of comfort, he said, "I am, however, tired of the country and intend to go to America for fresh lands and free institutions." He was delighted when we told him we were Americans and we satisfied as well as we could his eager enquiries about our country. When we proposed to go to Llangollen my feet were yet in a tub of cold water and Jones of the Priory said, "No sir, you shall not walk. You shall ride my cob," and the Irvings walking we proceeded to the village. The next morning we sent a card to the ladies of the Cottage, saying that three American gentlemen would be glad to look at it: receiving a favourable answer, we proceeded to this, one of the show places of the village. *The ladies,* known universally by that epithet, were a Miss Butler[61] and a Miss Ponsonby, two persons of good families and of wealth, who many years since fled clandestinely from the gay circles of Dublin to fix their residence in this secluded and beautiful valley. What motive of caprice or romance, prompted so strange a conduct, has not been disclosed. They were well educated and rich and are said to have been in early youth comely. She, the lady who received us at the door, had but few traces of grace or beauty. To our apology for the intrusion she said in a brusque voice, "Oh, all strangers like to see the old maids and the cottage. You are welcome, we are used to it. Look about to your hearts' content. The grounds and the two rooms are open to you. My friend is off on a ride, and when she returns I will mount and take my ride; don't think that your presence will incommode us—we are bred to it." The parlour was elegantly furnished, and still more elegantly an adjoining boudoir. Periodicals, prints, shew books and many nice little things were scattered about in profusion. While we were looking at the objects of curiosity, strutted into the room a fat clumsy old woman, in a cloth riding habit with a man's hat on her head, a large riding whip in her hand, and blurted out, "Miss Butler has received you—the *young* Lady of the Cottage. I have returned that I might assist in doing the honours of the house and letting her take her morning ride. We keep but one riding nag, and like Castor and Pollux we alternate." She walked about the room, slapping her riding skirt with her huge whip. "You are Americans," she said. "Bah—I have a view of Niagara, and a print of Washington,—those are your great things. One of your cards bore the name of Washington. I think he left no children." One of us said he was the father of his country. "You say true. He was a clever man. Our gracious Lord King George is hardly so clever. Gentlemen, join me in a glass of Shelton ale. I always take one glass after my ride." Any little romance about the ladies of the cottage had disappeared. The garden was small but exquisite. The Cerberus of a gardener growled, "Gentlemen, no flower is to be plucked. Mind ye." Hardly any degree of innate courtesy can survive the exposure to a perpetual intrusion of impertinent curiosity, to which show-places in Britain are subject but bruskery and swagger are surely offensive in the *Ladies* of the Cottage and bespeak a natural proclivity. I sent back to Jones of the Priory by the boy who took the horse our respective addresses with an intimation that if he came to America we should be glad to have notice of it. I have never since heard of him. All travelers in Wales mention the Ladies of the Cottage.

We visited Vale-Croce, went on to Holywell, stood on a rock whose haughty brow frowns over old Conway's roaring flood, had a distant view of Snowdon's height, lingered and loitered, and having rummaged Wales pretty well, we returned to Liverpool. Still Irving said to me "Your letters to London will keep.

Make that the last point of your tour, and you will see the people there to greater advantage the more you have seen elsewhere. Go there in the winter, take the fine season in the Country. Let us go to Scotland. Everybody is talking about the Lakes and all that, and September is the time to see them. When you have seen them and the highlands, you will be able to meet their lordships."

From Liverpool, there was easy access over delightful roads, thro a fine country, amidst exquisite rural scenery, to the Western and Central counties of England. Taking it as our *terminus a quo* we made excursions to many places of interest, for historic association, manufacturing activity, or beauty of scenery, and as for castles we I believe took [—?] every one in that whole region. We went to Sheffield, Preston and Manchester, to Stratford upon Avon, to Oxford, loitered a day in and about Warwick Castle, saw Kenilworth, Woodstock and Blenheim. Indeed pretty thoroughly pervaded that most lovely of all countries, where the magnificence of country palaces, the beauty and comfort of rural villages and cottages, the loveliness of landscapes, and all the appliances of civilization [are] more observed than in any other region of the earth. There are in England out of the Cities more stately palaces, more fine gardens, more pleasant and beautiful landscapes, more wealth and comfort, a more lavish and effective appropriation of money for the adornment and utilities of life than in any other country whatever. There are more palaces than in France, more good paintings than in Italy, more gardens than in Tuscany, and as for cottages they are not known out of England. Tho the Campagna Felix about Naples may in its small compass have more perfect objects to excite admiration, yet upon the whole that portion of England where the atmosphere is subject to the modifying influence of the Gulf Stream is the most delightful in the Autumnal months. While there is every thing to gratify the senses, there is nothing as in Italy to pain the heart. The beauty of still life is not meaner but on the contrary enhanced by the condition of man. There is not the languor inspiring fragrance of the orange grove, but the sweet smell of loaded hay. The peasant is not clad in the picturesque colours of the Italian, but he is clean and sturdy.

The time had come for our excursion to Scotland. Passing thro London hurriedly and incog.—that is not presenting our letters—we took the great northern road and reserving the numerous objects of interest, for a subsequent and more leisurely inspection,—a self denial requiring great effort, we hastened thro York and to Edinburgh. There it was our purpose notwithstanding the failure of our *pedestrian* excursion into Wales, to essay the highlands afoot. Peter Irving was no longer of our party, the company of Bardolph, Peto[62] and I was now reduced to two.

Washington Irving and I took the road for Stirling and the highlands.[63] Our first walk was to Linlithgow, an ancient Royal residence. We walked on steadily, and I flattered myself that I should be able to make the tour successfully. But at Linlithgow I found my feet again broken to pieces, and became assured of what experience has since confirmed, that my feet are disproportionately small and feeble for my size. The next morning they were swollen and inflamed, so of necessity I was compelled to adopt another mode of travelling to this and I hired a sort of large gig drawn by one horse in shafts, capable of holding two persons besides a small driver on a sort of stool in the front. Our driver was a small, red haired, freckled faced fellow 12 or 13 years old, smart, active and good tempered, capable of running by our side on rough or steep road, and always willing to urge the horse faster than we desired. The horse was a stout well set beast, of a grave temper, and not at all inclined to make speedy progress, nor were we inclined to exact it from him,—tho Kelty, as we called him, frequently called out as he trotted by our side, "Give him the whip, Gentlemen."

Bannockburn lay in our way. We of course paused to look at it. I think our minds were more full of the noble poem "Scots wha' hae" than with the battle itself. We saw the rock with a hole in it, in which it is said that Bruce fixed his standard. The fields were quiet under the calm sunlight, and the little brook murmured along, as it did on the day of battle, and will continue its liquid course unchanged, while land and rocks decay and change. I afterwards saw that same unchanging lapse in [—?] by [—?]

We were now in the region of Burns and Scott, and every stream and every rock was vocal with the voice of poetry. Soon

> Gray Stirling with her towers and town
> Upon our wending way looked down.

It was a bright sunset as up the flinty path we strained. The ascent was slow and toilsome so that it was not until the next morning that we could enjoy the glorious prospect from the Castle. We were in the midst of history and poetry—the feudal castle, the moat, the barbican, the palace of a rude and glittering royalty, on the edge of the lowlands and the highlands. From a feverish night we rose at the dawn, to behold the surrounding prospect. North we looked out beyond Callander, to the rugged highlands, on the other side upon the soft and unequalled beauties of the meadows amongst the links of Forth, the river, broad and deep, winding its way through involved mazes slowly as if loath to leave such fair lands. Amongst the links was plain to be seen, Cambus Kenneth gray—and onward little villages and mansions beautiful in the distance. I was pained to have obtruded upon my mind, the ill natured line— 'Far as the eye could reach no tree was seen,'— and I rejected it to think of the blue mountains, the green fields, the broad bright water and the touching poetry of bards and patriots that bathed the whole scene. Stirling detained us on its summit for two days rapturously spent. The two days' rest and the good fare had refreshed us as well as our steed Slug, and the boy Kelty. We went nearly thro Dunblane and Callander to Perth.

We decided to take the first canto of "The Lady of the Lake" (the Chase) as the programme of our route, and therefore went to Monan's hill and lone Glenartney's hazel shade, and we could not have made a better choice of a guide, for besides the poetical beauties of the exquisite poem, it is as exact in the description of the scenery and localities as the most minute and painstaking itinerary. In the most glowing and picturesque descriptions of Scott there is beyond any writer since Homer, a minute and accurate representation of real nature. His pictures are all portraits and hence the vividness with which they impress the imagination. We had in our hands "The Lady of the Lake" but the book was hardly necessary, for we knew the poem by heart. We set out at sunrise from Glenartney's hazel shade and having arranged with Kelty and his horse and gig to meet us wherever there was a road, we took the course of the Stag, only deviating from it when the ascents were too precipitous for us to climb. We passed round Benvoirlich, saw the Giant's den on Uam-Var, cooled ourselves amid the

> copsewood gray
> That waved and wept on Loch Achray.
> Where shall *we* find in foreign land
> So lone a Lake so sweet a strand.

The day had far advanced before the Bridge of Turk was seen, and Kelty and his horse as well as ourselves stood in need of refreshment. This we took on the margin of the stream spanned by the old bridge of Turk. Our refreshment was not confined to the cakes and ale we had brought along for that purpose, but stretching ourselves on the margent green we slumbered until it was too late to prosecute our inspection of the Trossachs, and at a short distance found very comfortable lodging in the hospitable mansion of Mr. James Stuart, a stalwart farmer somewhat above the rank of peasants. He said that Walter Scott's writings had brought so many of "you Southerners" to visit this region, that he had been compelled in self defence, and in charity to keep a sort of Inn. "But," said we, "we are not Englishmen but Americans." "Then," said he, "it shall not be an Inn for this night, but a highland cottage in which honoured guests are received by James Stuart," and surely no entertainment could have been more hospitable or comfortable. Our host, a most substantial Scotchman, was shrewd and intelligent. He told us that he was contemplating emigration to America, for which his enforced occupation for the last three years had provided him with the means. He told us many piquant anecdotes of English humorists, both men and women, said that Scott had once staid in his house two days and that notwithstanding his lame foot, he clambered thro the ravines and over the rocks as actively as "I or any highland Gilley."

At early morning we went under Stuart's guidance to explore the dangerous glen. It was as yet gloomy in the early day, the copsewood where the hunted stag had eluded his weary pursuers was pointed out, the loose shingly rocks over which the Gallant Gray had fallen. Here in this "darksome dell" in the deep "Trossachs' wilder nook," amidst cold dew and wild flowers, we hardly knew to which the greatest admiration was due, the exquisite beauties of the wild nature or the description of them in the Poem. Kelty said, "I think Slug is hardly as fine as that Gallant Gray you are reading about but I think he will go safe through." There stood before us the thunder-splintered pinnacle, near us were the ash and aspen, and I plucked a fox-glove the dust of which is yet between the leaves of my portfolio —put there in its bloom forty years ago.

> "Onward amid the copse gan peep
> A narrow inlet still and deep—

and on it, strange to say, were a pair of small wild ducks. The illusion was so strong that when a short space onward I saw the water of the Lake, I looked to see the Lady of the Lake in her light shallop. With a sort of enthusiasm I stepped forward to the pebbled margin and took a hearty draught of the water. The space of water to the Island seemed an hundred yards or thereabouts. In a moment I was stripped, with the purpose of swimming over where the borderman and Malcolm Graeme had swam, and there was in full view the identical oak behind which Duncraggan's withered dame had stood, when amidst the storm she had dealt the fatal dagger blow to the adventurous spearman. I found the water of the Lake very cold, but I soon accomplished the enterprize. As I stood beside the oak Irving called across to me, "Preston, you may out-swim me, but remember I can out-walk you." I waved adieux to Mr. James Stuart, and Irving quickly crossing in a skiff, we spent the day in rummaging the Island. There was a fantastical little boat house, most inappropriately erected on it, where skiffs were kept for hire. Since that time still more inappropriately has been put upon the Lake a small steam boat, called the Ellen Douglas!! but in our explorations, I think we discovered the identical old tree described by Scott against which Allan Bayne reclined, as blasted, worn and gray as he. I can't but think that this old tree suggested that beautiful picture. Every touch of his pencil draws a real object, and every inspiration springs from nature.

From Loch Katrine we passed over to Loch Lomond, afoot thro a somewhat desolate and monotonous valley. There were observable some small objects of interest, obscure remains of forts or towers, but Rob Roy's cave was in our way and there we paused, for whatever has been touched by Scott, has attractive associations. The valley seen under a bright sunshine had a solitary and quiet aspect that was striking. Irving stopped to note what constituted the particulars. He noted the sunshine, the silence, the gray mountain sides, a few patches of Bracken, a pile of rocks, as it might be the foundation of an old tower, the absence of all sign of animal life, but the distant crowing of a cock, which he said made the scene much more solitary. Tho we sailed near the cove of Ben Lomond, we were content to leave its vast heights unattempted and drifted slowly down the Lake, a wide expanse of water, to the Leven Water, the place of Smollett's birth, and to Dunbarton town and castle. Thence to Greenoc and Glasgow. From the latter city we took a new departure into the land of Burns, to Auld Ayre, which nere a town surpasses for honest men and bonny lasses. We took the memorable road of Tam O'Shanter, saw Kirk Alloway, and with reverence and awe, saw the humble mansion, where was born the greatest British poet since Shakespeare, we saw old Ailsa and Bonny Doon, and had occasion to remark that on the coast of Ayreshire, there were the most beautiful sunsets we had ever seen. There was a flood of tender light upon the sea, the fields, the villages, the equal of which I have never witnessed since, not in Italy or South Carolina.

Returning to London I encountered in the Saloon of Covent Garden, my college mate Mr. Govan[63a] just beginning an European tour. In a few days we arranged to make together the trip upon the Continent. We fell acquainted too with Mr. Campbell of Virginia, who had come over to have a son born to him in Scotland, in which count an inheritance was to be cast upon him. Mr. Campbell being in poor health, he was going to spend the winter in France.

Crossing to Calais to our great surprize Govan and I were arrested on account of some suspected informality in our passports. A very polite officer told us that he was sorry that we must be restricted within the fortifications of the town until he could receive further orders from Paris, and added, "If you are Americans, as you purport to be, you had best let me send with my dispatch a letter from you to your Ambassador." We agreed to avail ourselves of his politeness, and he requested that the letter might be an open one. The very polite official after some conversation stated to us that the police were on the *qui vive* for the return from America of some French refugees, M. Leniere Demouetti[?], and some body else whose name I have forgotten, but that he not doubting that we were what we represented ourselves to be, would only restrict us from going into the Country, and allow us to walk if we so wished on the outer walls and within view of an officer of the police. All this was very polite and annoying and a sudden and thorough initiation into a system very different from anything we had ever seen. The sense of restraint and surveillance was very galling. The three or four days were spent heavily enough, principally in walking upon the outward ramparts, and looking restlessly over the fields and along the road to Paris. But beside our initiation into a novel restraint upon our free actions, a very capital hotel invited us into the pleasures of a French *Cuisine,* a pleasant mystery unknown in any other country and in one's immediate adaptation to which is proved how high art is in conformity to nature. We furbished up our small French vocabulary by talking to every body willing to talk with us, and the French are not unwilling to indulge a foreigner in this exercise. Notwithstanding the multitude of English who frequent the place, it seemed to us the habitual (perhaps natural) politeness of the population was not impaired. In this change we found some solace for our detention. At length came the permission to proceed from the office of police and a polite note from Mr. Gallatin.[64] The same officer who had arrested us came with many professions of politeness and sorrow,—that what he was pleased to call the unnecessary sensibility of the police had made it his unpleasant duty etc., and really spoke so blandly that our leave taking was rather that of friends with mutual kindness than of prisoners and jailers.

The scene upon which we entered was entirely novel, the huge lumbering and awkward Diligense looking like a traveling village drawn by coarse, long tailed, rough haired stallions, ungroomed and harnessed in the most outré fashioned rope traces, painted wooden hames, rising high above the horses' withers and decorated with red fustian strings. The drivers were two postilions, immersed up [to] the groin, in a receptacle called Jack boots, each driver armed with a great whip, which he smacked like the crack of a pistol. As we left the hotel a little dog jumped up behind the postilion and barked fiercely as we rattled over the rough pavement. It seemed as if the croaking, rattling and shaking machine would tumble to pieces, and discharge the population assembled on the wheels—but amidst apparent confusion and disorder, we made the five miles an hour with great punctuality and were subjected to no mishap, to the cats, dogs, children, bird cages, and flower pots that made up our miscellaneous freight. There was much drinking of wine, eating of cakes, and when it was known that we were not Englishmen, there was infinite fun and laughter. How different the establishment of the English mail coach with its elegant well groomed horses, drawn up, the four into the smallest possible space, under the guidance of a slight set of reins, held by a well dressed coachman on the box,—the coach, an elegant piece of machinery,—the harness well fitted and strong with a minuteness that but for the contrary experience, would not seem to be stout enough for its purpose,—the running gear, looking like a model machine in a work shop, the whole turn out, most compact, trim, finished and appropriate, making ten miles an hour, without any interference on the part of the driver; within, the passengers quiet, clean and glum, sitting bolt upright with an umbrella standing between their legs, and ever and anon passing the hand along that side of the thigh next a fellow passenger to prevent contact with him. It was in the night that we got to the city. Through gloomy, noiseless and darksome streets, we drove to our hotel. The scant furniture and uncarpeted rooms gave an air of discomfort, enhanced by the floors being of porcelain. But the next morning the glories of the Rue de la Paix and of the Place Vendôme dispelled all care for comfort. Mr. Gallatin and Mr. Burnet, the consul, were as civil as possible, but the attentions to me of Mr. Warden,[64a] ex-consul des Etats Unis,[65] were such that, soon an intimacy sprung up between us.

It would be vain and endless to speak of Paris. All the world knows it. I confine myself to things personal to myself. I found my friend and kinsman James Brown,[65a] afterwards Ambassador to France, in the City. Legaré[66] came in a few days. Legaré had come over with Dr. Raoul as a fellow passenger with whom he had all the time talked in French, and thus besides his facility of learning, spoke much more fluently and correctly than either of us. We all desired to acquire fluency and Legaré wished to learn to speak elegantly. To this end, Mr. Warden procured from a literary lady friend of his permission to dine daily with her and her family, where the conversation should be entirely in French. The family consisted of the Lady Mother, a very accomplished woman who had been familiar in the literary and political circles of the late régime, and of three daughters, Inez, a favourite pupil of Isabey[67] the painter, of Osama, taking lessons in declamation from

Talma[68] and Mademoiselle Duchesnoise[69] and of Natalie the youngest, who was taking lessons and a proficient in music.

Madame D'Epinarde was the widow of a gentleman, somewhat known in literature as the author of a long poem on Commerce. He had been sent on embassy to Murat at Naples, and on leaving that city had died suddenly, as it was suspected, by foul means. During the Bonaparte ascendancy the widow enjoyed a pension, which of course ceased upon the restoration, and now in straightened circumstances, was not unwilling to be assisted in the maintenance of the family by having three gentlemen at her table, recommended as *gentlemen* by her friend Mr. Warden,—the daily 20 francs, being a fair compensation in the judgment of that gentleman. The regulations of the household were stately and somewhat elegant. Dinner punctually at 6 o'clock, the family and the guests in dress. In the beginning of the second week Madame D'Epinarde said, "Mr. Legaré, you will please to take a seat by Mademoiselle Osama, you, Mr. Govan, by Mlle. Inez, and you, Mr. Preston, here between me and Natalie and this arrangement will continue as long as we have the honor of your being with us. That vacant plate is for Mr. Warden when he may chose to favour us with his company or for Mr. Talma when he chooses to dine quietly with an old friend, preparing for an unusual effort." Very often, indeed more frequently than otherwise, we chose to dine at a restaurant or other place, always giving notice of this intention as early as possible to our hostess. There were frequent little gatherings of an evening—

occasionally Talma or Mars[70] or Duchesnoise, members of the Imperial or Republican parties. Amongst the visitors I remember Benjamin Constant, Mr. Scheffer,[71] Lafayette's friend, and there were swarms of journalists and pamphleteers. Madame D'Epinarde had a free ticket to the Theatre Francaise. We frequently went thither and to the other theatres and places of amusement. When at home of an evening, Osama would declaim from the tragedies and Natalie play upon all sorts of instruments, and I occasionally recited for them passages from Shakespeare or other English poets. The Lady and Natalie understood and spoke English very well. Legaré's French was the subject of much commendation by the lady. "You, Mr. Preston, do not make so much progress; is it that Natalie is a bad teacher, or as I suspect that you are vain of your speaking of your vernacular? I have observed that in persons who thought well of their speaking. How is it Mr. Legaré?" *"Vous y êtes,"* said Legaré—it is not Mademoiselle Natalie's fault but his vanity." "But," said she, "I think Mr. Legaré sets up to be correct in his own language." "I suspect—Vous y êtes," said I, in my turn.

Warden at that time was busily engaged on his work and I was much with him during the composition. To my surprise he inclosed in the book a letter from me in which I had at his request furnished him with information of the Missouri and Mississippi which I had derived from Governor Clark on my visit to St. Louis. The introduction to the work was written by Verplanck.

While on her visit to Paris Lady Morgan was an

habitué of Mdme. D'Epinarde's house. In fact Warden, who was gouty and stiff, in some sort turned her ladyship over to me, to go about with her. Her manners were free according to my American taste. One day leading her down stairs from Madame D'Epinarde's, she stopped me on the landing and raising her veil, said, "Mr. Preston, is there rouge enough on my left cheek?" "Very little," I told her. "Then," said she, "stop here until I go back to the mirror and put a little more." When that ferocious and blackguard review of her *France* came out in the *Quarterly*[72] she was affected to tears with rage and shame. She asked me, "Are those books of which I speak[73] of the character that the reviewer attributes to them?" "I am ashamed," I replied, "that I know them to be so." "I was led into the mistakes," she said, "by that vile roué Lord Blessington, and deserve the mortification for having had acquaintance with such a brute. Are you sure," said she, "that *bouquets d'arbres*"[74] occurs in 'Paul and Virginia'? Show it to me and I will track Croker lined [?] 'with St. Pierre,' which may perhaps beat some brains into the unmannerly dog."

Being known as a kinsman of Mr. Brown, whose talents, high standing in the Senate of the United States, and whose perfect fluency in the French language gave him a position in society, I enjoyed some advantages from it. Indeed it had come to be whispered, as I learned from Mr. Gallatin, that Brown would probably [be] his successor at that court, and that I might possibly be an attaché of the embassy. Thus when there was a dinner at the Duke de Richelieu's[75] preliminary to a conference of the Savants about weights and measures [I was invited]. The Duke was at that time prime Minister. The whole invited party of eleven were at the door as the bell struck six and we all walked in together. The Duke received us in the Parlour; there was no introduction of any one except that Gallatin said—"Your Grace, my young countryman from Virginia." In a very few minutes, the door opened, and we went to table. I did not perceive any order in the mode of placing the guests, unless it were that Mr. Brown had his seat at the Duke's right and M. Dumont[76] and myself found ourselves together at the opposite end. On the other side of the Duke was Pozzo di Borgo,[77] and La Place,[78] a litle old man in black, was about midway the table. I do not remember that La Place talked at all. Pozzo di Borgo spoke most frequently and as it seemed to me just as it happened in French, Italian, or English. The main topic of conversation was as to the mode of organizing a Congress to consider about a uniformity of weights and measures. There was no continuous or regular conversation. Many remarks were made and apparently slight suggestions. "In such a Congress," said the Duke, slightly bowing to Gallatin and Brown, "America must be strongly represented, she having so large an experience of the decimal deficiencies." "I fear," said the Duke, "we can hardly organize the Congress until next year." Of all the men that it has been my fortune to see, the Duke de Richelieu struck me as the most perfect specimen of an elegant gentleman, an elegant person and countenance, noble physiognomy, graceful manners—

gracious aspect and perfect bienseance, nor have I in after life met with anything comparable to that dinner in all its appurtenances. It struck me as having been perfect, except that there was no lady. As in leaving the table Pozzo di Borgo passed my chair, he said to me, as I rose to bow to him,—"Vous êtes monsieur de la Province de Virginia." "No Sir, of the State." "Hah," said he, with somewhat a doubtful smile, "de l'état."

Mr. Gallatin was conspicuously kind to me. I frequently dined with him and was of all his parties. His standing as a man of talents and information was very high. His family in America was a distinguished one. There were two of his cousins in France at that time representing two Courts. Gallatin with all his ability was not enough *American* for his station. When on one occasion Mr. Gallatin was called from his table leaving Dumont and myself, Dumont alluding to a conversation respecting Washington, Chief-Justice Marshall, and American men and affairs, said, "You and Mr. Gallatin seem to differ a good deal." "Yes," said I, "I am an American." "I perceive the difference," said he.

Dumont was a professed Literateur, editor and commentator, indeed supposed to be the writer of many pieces published in the name of Bentham. Certain it is that the French exposé of the Benthamite doctrines was much more elegant than the English. He was Republican in his principles, a great admirer of American institutions, and not a little scandalized at old Gallatin's *non* Americanisms. Gallatin never spoke morally of Washington and as to Franklin, he habitually called him (with my entire assent) "the old fox"—an epithet that was not inappropriate to Gallatin himself.

Dumont was the redacteur of Jeremy Bentham's works, which being written in the absurd dialect called by the wits of that day the Benthamese, were *translated* (as Dumont modestly professed) but in fact reproduced in elegant French and thus obtained some currency on the Continent.

My old friend Dr. Cooper[79] was a great admirer of Bentham and induced me to read his works in after life, which I did with some profit and little pleasure. They have greatly fallen into disuse.

Mrs. Gallatin was a very plain Pennsylvania matron, good and unpretending. Upon occasion of a ball given by the Duke of Wellington she was exceedingly worried by the numerous and urgent application of her countrymen to her to procure tickets for them. The pertinacity of the applications was vexatious. The old lady was greatly embarrassed. What was to be done? Certain principles were decided on, which being somewhat in conformity to supposed court rules, might obtain acquiescence. I had been admitted to the council as one who knew most of the Americans. First it was resolved that those could not be invited who had not been presented to the King. This cut off a good many, for Gallatin had incurred some odium by his reluctance to present rag-tag and bob-tail at Court. Then it was decided that those who had not been presented to the President of the United States could not have tickets begged for them. These principles and the cry of shame which we raised against the indecent and unrepublican eagerness to get into an aristocratic party left on Mrs. Gallatin's hands, a comparatively small number to be offended, and of those whose vainness was gratified by being at the ball, they paid amply in the disrespect of their countrymen. Our countrymen have a preëminent and indecent propensity to thrust themselves upon exclusive circles, to seek the acquaintance of distinguished and above all titled people, and in the indulgence of this appetite, they often trample upon rules of propriety and expose themselves to disparaging remarks. In regard to nobility our people have a rapturous and romantic regard for it. It is one of the hereditary feelings of our blood, and with us exaggerated because we know nothing of it in its reality and *omne ignotum pro magnifico.* Of all the people in Paris our Yankees were most concerned about the Wellington ball, envious of those who had the good fortune of the *entrée,* and curious as to what took place in the mysterious and magnificent interior. Those who had meanly begged and almost fought their way in, gave us pompous accounts of the gorgeous scenes, with amiable consideration for those who had had the misfortune to be absent. It was some compensation to us, when sometime afterwards, Lafette the Banker gave a ball in emulation of the Duke's, and from the fact of holding our funds bid us to it. It was a grand entertainment—a huge crowd, and characterized as I have never failed to see even at the best ordered entertainments, [by] a hubbub and a rush at supper. The most striking spectacle of the occasion was the entry of old Prince Esterhazy,[80] a little old man with a purple velvet frock coat and breeches bedizened with jewels and attended closely by two pages, who went with him from supper thro the rooms, slowly and solemnly, a lane being provided for him. It was whispered that the pages were intended to protect him from having a diamond plucked from his clothes, or to pick them up if they fell. His breast was in a blaze of jewelled orders.

Genl. Lafayette was of the party. He was very polite to me whenever he was in Paris. I saw a good deal of him. He was indeed paterfamilias to the Americans. He at one time was somewhat in trouble about his friend Scheffer, who having written an offensive pamphlet, was condemned to deportation and a fine. This the general thought it his duty to pay and we his children, thought it our duty to relieve him from a small subscription amongst us sufficed to effect this. The hospitalities I received from the illustrious old gentleman I was in some sort able to return or rather to manifest my sense of when upon his visit to the United States,[81] Governor Manning[82] assigned to me as his chief aid the command of the escort to receive him at the North Carolina line, and conduct him to Columbia the Capital. As the North Carolina cortège brought the General to the line at the head of our column, the Genl. extended his hand to me and said, "I am too happy that your Governor has thought proper to confide his authority on this pleasing occasion to one whom I remember with so much pleasure in Paris. Please, Col. Preston, if your duties permit, take a seat with me in the carriage and we will have a talk of old times." I had a squadron of cavalry under the immediate command of Col. Deas, several companies of light troops and many militia companies, tapering off into a countless multitude of men, women and children. All should welcome Lafayette, and pressed to gaze upon his beloved person. Our sluggish movement threw us late at night when we got to Cheraw. The road for miles was lit up with bonfires, casting their lights amongst the tall pines. When we got near Cheraw, Genl. David R. Williams met us with large concourse and said, "We have not been able to find a revolutionary soldier to head this procession, so the people brevetted me one, and sent me as a representative." "Alas," said the General, "my brethren in arms are almost all gone but I am happy to see their children." "And their children happy to see you," said Williams, and the shout extended away off into the darkness which covered the end of the line.

From Cheraw our next encampment was at Lovick Young's on Lynch's Creek, where every tree and bush as far as the eye could reach was illuminated. The feasting and shouting and revelry had not subsided at midnight when Col. Deas, an officer of punctilious military etiquette, came in and enquired "At what hour in the morning is it your pleasure that the tents be struck?" "Please take your orders, Col. Deas, from Genl. Lafayette." The Genl. said, "As it is but a short and smooth march to Camden we will begin it as late as 9 o'clock that the troops may have time to make themselves comfortable"—but I am seduced into this episode. *Revenons à nos moutons,* that is being interpreted, let's go from the piney woods of South Carolina, five years back to Paris.

Almost the whole time that I was there, I spent every morning except Saturday in the Bibliothèque du Roy. As soon as it was perceived that I was an habitué my chair and place at the table seemed to be reserved for me and the officials of the room saluted me on a morning when I came in. I read assiduously four hours every day, from nine to one, and then went a sight-seeing. The Louvre Gallery yet blazed with the glories of art brought to that place from all parts of Europe. I soon learned enough to discriminate and to enjoy the Italian school of painting,—in the contemplation of which I found great delight. Stewart Newton and Leslie[82a] and occasionally Mamselle Inez were there copying, and they were pleased with that amiability which belongs to artists, to encourage and inform my nascent taste. The French style of art in all its manifestations was unpleasant to me, the Dutch painters not at all agreeable and least of all Rubins, but the Italian a perpetual glory to my imagination, first the Roman and then the other schools. My natural taste for statuary was perhaps stronger than for painting. My emotion of delight in beholding at Wrexham in Wales that first piece I ever saw,[83] either created a taste or raised an instinct which I have felt ever since, and I recognized the same sort of emotion when I came to see the *Apollo* at the Vatican.

In Paris there is every where a vast deal of fine art, rarely attaining the highest excellence but so diffused as to affect the whole surface of life. It is delightful to look upon, and if on the one hand the sensuousness of Paris has a tendency to sensuality, on the other it has a decided tendency and a near approximation to the imaginative. If Civilization is the abounding of demand and supply, a multitude of wants and their gratification, and this may be true when we consider our whole complex nature, sensitive, intellectual and moral, then Paris is at the head of Civilization. What is the highest and best state of Civilization—may be a question—perhaps it is a just combination of those qualities of our nature as regards their wants and gratification. In Paris I suspect the senses and the intellect have perhaps an undue preponderance. The pleasures of each are almost unlimited.

The days passed thus, some hours in the Bibliothèque du Roy, with half a million of books, a stroll on the Boulevards, thence to the Louvre with its pictures and statues—a dinner with artists or savants or what was better with Madame D'Epinarde, and the young ladies, in the evening to hear Talma or Duchesnoise or Mars at the Theatre.

My progress in speaking French was not great. In truth my instructress, little Natalie, learned English so rapidly that our talk was a good deal in that tongue. It was sweet to hear the scarcely perceptible accent of the French girl, as she exhibited her accomplishment to new acquaintances. She was a very charming girl. When we came to part, it was not without emotion. At that time she had a declared suitor, a Sir James Stuart, who as it seemed to me was favoured by the mother perhaps more than by the daughter. We parted with regret, but with no intimation of the possibility of our meeting again, which indeed turned out so.

One meets with odd little adventures in Paris. There was a negro man named Jack who attached himself pertinaciously to me and Legaré and became a real attaché. He had been brought over from Charleston as a servant to an old blind Jew named Sasportas, who upon being couched and restored to his sight dismissed Jack, according to contract, with a month's wages. One evening in the Palais Royal, we met Jack, who having known Legaré in Charleston rushed upon him like a lost dog who finds his master, and caressing and fawning upon him, manifested the utmost delight, declaring that he had not eaten for some days, for altho he had eight dollars in his pocket, he could not ask for anything to eat, as these folks understood nothing but their own gibberish. Thenceforward Jack made a trio with us and always compared whatever he saw in Paris disparagingly with what was in Charleston. Thus it happened that one early morning we were walking thro the Place Vendôme when the morning rays had about half descended the bronze Column, in the center, and were tinging the tall houses on the opposite side, we having from our stand point a glimpse of the sun shine on the Tuillieres garden. I turned to Jack and said, "You rascal, did you ever seen any thing as beautiful as this?" He quickly answered, "Mars Preston, all very pretty, but were you ever in Charleston, up towards Cooter Bridge?" Several years after Legaré and I went to explore Jack's high place at Cooter Bridge. There were a few wooden shanties by the side of a canal filled with green water,—but it was Jack's birth place.

I received a note signed Sam. Coles, saying that having heard from Mr. Burnet his friend of my being in Paris he would call on me as a countryman. With a family of that name I was connected, and expected to meet a kinsman. When the gentleman presented himself, I learned that this shortly was his history. He was the son of a blacksmith, living two miles west of Salem, had seen me once at his father's shop, that having made some money, he invested it in bacon to curry on salt at the Kanawha Saltworks, that he could not sell it for cash and took the value in salt. This salt he took to Louisville, which he was then compelled to reconvert into bacon, this he took in a boat purchased by him to New Orleans. There he bartered his bacon for cotton, and put it on board a vessel going to Havre—taking charge of his freight himself. At Havre he fell into some difficulty with the Custom house, and came up to Paris to see sights and Mr. Gallatin. Our acquaintance rapidly progressed into familiarity. He had got a servant at his hotel to go about with him and having enough money he suffered for nothing except that the victuals he got looked and tasted very suspicious. He had pleaded in vain for bacon and greens, for which he paid [?]. I was able to take him to [a] restaurant where calling for *salé aux choux*, the demanded dish was set before him to his great delight. It was as good an article of the kind as was ever put on a table in Virginia. Coles was a rough, shrewd, self-dependent and fearless fellow. Not much given to admiration—and always saying straightforward what he thought or felt. We were very much together for a couple of weeks. With plenty of money and a native hardihood of character, he had no *mannière haute* or affectation. When we were looking at Bigottini[84] dancing, he said to me, "Preston, it's a damned shame here before all these ladies," and when the spectacle closed he said, "It is altogether fantastical and only fit for a despotism." Odd things in Paris where there are so many such do not in general attract remark, but Cole's peculiarity of dress and manners as he sat familiarly with a young gentleman fashionably dressed, and having as I flattered myself an air de bonne ton, did attract attention, for I perceived that we were the subject of curious observation. Coles bought a supply of mantles, cloaks and other gay articles on which as I afterwards understood he had made a good adventure at New Orleans. What became of him I have never learned. Leslie and Stuart Newton and my friend Petticolas made many drawings of him. They were always sketching. On the back of a card they would make a rough sketch and finish it off when we got home.

Catalani[85] was singing at the opera, Bigottini was dancing, Talma, Duchesnoise, and Mars were acting. Burnet was also on the stage. Every day there were fresh caricatures in the shop windows of *Les Anglaises pour[elles-]mêmes*. My dress and complexion being English, (The London tailors had a higher reputation than those of Paris) I was occasionally saluted by a gruff *Goddamn*. On one occasion a little fellow ran against me and roughly exclaimed "Goddamn." I thrust him with some violence against the walk, the rencontre making an ally in the crowd. While the petit maître recovered himself, a police officer said, "Sir, I saw it. He was an impertinent." I said, "I am no Englishman, but an American." "Pass on," said the policeman. The hatred of the English was intense,—breaking thro the habitual politeness of the people. It was manifested every where, on the theatre, at the shop windows, amongst the people. For the first time the bienséance of the nation gave way in a retort upon the habitual and hereditary rivalry of the English against the French. The French have not equal talent with the English for caricature, but their exact and perfect portraiture of the English was a most piquant caricature of their awkwardness, ungainliness and gruffness, especially of the women. An English woman is the perfection of gaucherie and a French woman of elegance—a gracefulness of manner and propriety of dress are diffused through all ranks. My blanchisseuse* (I am afraid to put the English word) was always costumé with a propriety and beauty, and especially harmony of colours. Petticolas made her a study—She was very prosperous in her trade, had many employes under her, —kept her accounts neatly in a little set of books,—she was 23 years old—had saved some money to invest in a shop. On her marriage, with Victor, my barber, a most excellent young man, I was bidden to the wedding by an elegant point note accompanied by a barber. The dress, manners, and general appearance of the numerous assembly at the marriage seemed to me to be equal to any party of ladies and gentlemen that I had ever seen or have seen.

Some lessons from an Italian master had enabled me to read that language and Natalie said that my attempts to speak it were more successful than those at French. So we arranged that Govan, Mr. Brown, his wife, and myself should be of a party to Italy. Govan and I bought a great strong ugly carriage of Russian structure called a Bradshaw. We hired a valet de voyage, named Fabre, a native of Pisa, who spoke all the continental languages, was an accomplished servant and a great rogue. Brown had also a servant. In posting, therefore, we generally had the same number of horses to our carriages, being two; sometimes, however, we were condemned to four, and Brown, who was a man of stately and dignified manner and had besides a lady was sometimes taxed with six. We took the road for Marseilles, pretty much the same that Gray and Walpole had taken in 1739, nearly a hundred years ago and which is so exquisitely described in Gray's letters to Mr. West, his father and mother, letters which I think the most elegant of any in our language from gentlemen. Lady Mary's[86] beat them and hers I think alone. I say in our language, for in the French there are many equal. We went through Rheims to Dijon and Lyons, posting when en route some sixty or eighty miles a day.

We never stopped at an inn without having made specific bargain for every article, first two rooms with two beds in each, for so Brown and his wife required, à la Francaise, the dishes required at the meals, and special permission secured to buy our own wine. Fabre arranged all this before we entered the house and as we knew always exacted a douceur for himself.

From Lyons we took the road to Geneva, making the mountainous passage of the Alps, traversed by a magnificent road made by that wonderful man Napoleon, a road comparable to, indeed surpassing the noble specimens of this kind in ancient Italy. Each carriage had six horses, though four would have been entirely sufficient. The grade of the road was easy and its surface perfectly smooth as a garden walk. It passed thro walls of snow, on either side of from 10 to 20 feet high. Every half mile, there was a substantial building, with several rooms, which was occupied by a sentinel, to furnish assistance to travellers in case of accident. The road forty feet wide was either cut into the solid rock, or carried upon galleries made of solid masonry. We endeavored to identify or imagine, the place where Mr. Walpole's little black spaniel had been seized by the wolf as recounted in Gray's letter,[87] but we [neither] passed through nor near any clump of pines. We staid all night in a little miserable village called Lanslebourg almost a waste of snow. There was but one Inn and we were released from the necessity of driving a bargain for our fare by the fact that it was regulated by the police of the road. I believe that every inhabitant of the village had a *goitre*, even children. Our lodgings were comfortable and cheap, nor did we experience cold here as we walked out on the crusted ice. We perceived the thin air of the mountain top, but not unpleasantly.

At the point at which we began to descend the

Southern declivity of the mountain, the post master insisted that we should continue to take six horses in our carriages which were not only useless but, as it seemed to me, dangerous. On the steep descent along the frequent windings of the road I remonstrated, but he insisted. I said that I stood in no need of the horses which would indeed be a dangerous encumbrance to me, but he replied, "Those who come up the mountain require that many to convey them to this post." The controversy became warm and angry. Fabre flew into a towering passion—exhausted the profuse vocabulary of Italy in swearing,—pointing to the gilt tassel in my cap, he said, "Don't you see he is a Russian officer?" "If he were the Czar," said the post master, "he shall take six horses," and was proceeding to attach the two horses to the carriage, when I thrust the groom aside with violence, and said, "I will walk to Susa and leave the carriage here until I can send the police for it." This induced a pause and a truce in which a compromise was effected. I agreed to pay for the six horses, without taking them, and paid a dollar to the groom whom I had pushed, but he swore I had struck. Peace being thus happily restored, we descended merrily and rapidly, catching occasional glimpses of the plains of Italy, and at every moment perceiving the influence of a warmer climate. At Susa, climate, landscape and all proclaimed that we were in Italy and above all a beautiful girl whom I saw sewing at a window,—the carriage was very near the house—As she threw back her long black curls to look at the travellers, I raised my cap and bowed,— and a smile prompted me on the sudden to jump out the carriage and enter the room, where sat the fair Italian girl and her mother. My entrance was of course somewhat awkward,—and the ladies manifestly enjoyed it. I said, "I am a foreigner, have come to see the beauties of Italy, and this is the first that has attracted me." My speech, flurried, was of course very outré, the old lady handed me a book from a chair, which I found to be, Conversations in French and Italian, the two languages in opposite columns. The young lady was studying French. The contemplations of the book were exactly to the purpose, and I had a most pleasant half hour's talk, which Mr. Brown broke in upon, saying, "If you stop for every pretty thing you meet with in Italy we will never get on." Asking a thousand pardons for my brusque intrusion which were politely and gracefully granted by the ladies, they asked me to leave my card, and said they would keep it. "That is a nicer adventure," said Mr. Brown, "than that of Mr. Walpole's black spaniel."

Night was closing when we passed Rivoli; it was long after dark when we got to Turin. The next morning by sunup I went out to look upon the Po-Pater Eridanus—and walking on its bank, I met a friar in a tippet cloak with a long beard. After we had passed each other for some steps, both turning we again met. The friar said, "You are a stranger, Sir, apparently looking at the river." "Yes, I am a foreigner, and see it for the first time." "You are an Englishman." "No Sir." "A Russian?" "No Sir." "A German?" "No Sir." "Of what country may I be so bold as to ask?" "An American." "Hah," said he, as he stepped back, and regarded me from head to foot. "I have never seen an American before, and yet you are my compatriot, for your country was discovered by an Italian and I too am a Genoese," whereupon he threw his arms round me, with a sort of ecstasy as if he had found a treasure. We walked up and down the banks for an hour. I was his first American, and he my first friar. His convent was on the opposite side of the river on the brow of a high hill descending sheer to the stream, a beautiful site commanding a view of the beautiful city and river. The acquaintance thus fortunately made, procured me the pleasure of a daily visit from the good brother and several of the brethren of his convent, during the days we continued in Turin. Being in the gallery one day looking at the pictures a sentinel rushed in crying, "Clear the gallery. The King[88] is coming." I fled precipitately and in my flight had nearly rode over his Majesty at the moment ascending the stairs. I heard the King say as [I] hurriedly passed, "An Englishman." "No," I cried, "an American." My friar strangely enough turned out to be a thorough Bonapartist—and most of his monks. He told me that the King was a great fool, that upon his restoration he had abolished every thing that had transpired during his exile and that to pacify the State he and his convent, had walked round the palace three times chanting a *te deum* and sprinkling themselves and the walls with holy water, whereupon it was announced that there was a purification of the premises from the contamination of the usurpers, that old things were done away with and a new order, or rather the ancient order, which had been interrupted, reëstablished. His Majesty passing through the Museum was asked if he would not step in and see the ornithological collection. "No," said he, "I don't like any of those vile painted things of the French usurpation. Take me to look at the birds, of which I understand you have a great many." So "ornithology" over the door was hastily painted out and "Birds" put in the place.

I had determined for my own satisfaction and perhaps that of my friends to keep a journal of my travels thro Italy, to make some sketch of objects which particularly interested me and to mark the emotions with which they affected me and this I sedulously set about. But I soon found that my routine of life and experiences were precisely those that had already been recorded an hundred times with all the elegance of description and minuteness of detail possible. We had a wide assortment that had been written, from Addison down to the recent elaborate and elegant Nash Eustace's "Italian Tour." Govan particularly amused himself with a frivolous and flashy work of the Abbé Du Pattais, full of declamatory affectation, and most ridiculous extravagancies and yet indicating a shrewd and keen observation of nature and art. All that I could touch or think or see was thus anticipated, and the record was always in reach. Thus in recording my reminiscences other than of incident purely personal, I should find myself repeating in a less agreeable manner what may be found in Addison or Dr. More's view of society and manners in Italy or in Eustace or a thousand other books. I shall therefore do now, what I did in that journal, note my route of travel, with little else.

Turin with many attractions in and about it, in the regularity of its plan, and wonderful cleanliness and neatness puts one in mind of Philadelphia—and there is a further resemblance as to the beautiful plain in which it is situated and the noble river near it. The Schuylkill and the Po, are much alike,—but Philadelphia lacks that barrier of hills, upon the top of the highest one of which was situated the Monastery of my friend the Genoese friar. In this asylum neither he or his confreres knew any thing of America since the days of Columbus,—except that part of it was a dependence of England and a part of Spain. There were but few interesting specimens of art in Turin, few paintings and fewer statues. The climate was exquisite. A week was spent here delightfully.

Leaving Turin, we passed the Trebia, famous for a battle between Hannibal and the Roman Consul. The rivel was in flood from recent rains, and altho a wide and shallow stream the current was so strong that to prevent the carriage from being washed off it was necessary that a half a dozen stout fellows should wade along to hold it. Govan and I took Mrs. Brown into our carriage. Brown and the servants took the other. We had proceeded but a short distance, when the stream was pouring through the carriage and we felt that it was yielding to the current. Govan leapt out to help hold it, and he and the six naked Italians, most stalwart fellows, were able to effect it, but Mrs. Brown in her fright could not refrain from looking out, where those bronze figures were battling and struggling amidst the water. It certainly was not a spectacle exactly fit for the eyes of a timid lady, and when we had happily attained the shore, her fear was immediately transformed into rage that I had brought her into such a predicament. In the process of dressing, however, for which purpose she used a tire room made by the two carriages formed into a sort of apartment, she became calm and joined us in a bottle of wine to make merry on our adventurous passage of the Trebia. The scant raiment of our Italian guards had been brought over by one of their party on the top of a pole so that they were in a few moments in presentable trim to receive thanks and double pay, which last circumstance induced one of them to offer an Elephant's tooth which he said had been picked up in the neighborhood, and he said had doubtless been a tooth of one of Hannibal's elephants. I thought it probable and gave him 20 francs for it. It is now in Dr. Gibbes' collection of curiosities in Columbia.[89]

The approach to Rome has been described by a thousand writers. The desolate campagne which surrounds it is very sad and lonely. It is fit to inspire and a most [proper] accompaniment for those thoughts which oppress the mind, as one approaches the sepulchre of nations. The emotions are solemn and awful. Silence and lifelessness is all around; an occasional glimpse of the dome of St. Peter's is an incongruous object, for it is of actual existence not of the past. It does not harmonize with primeval emotions. It obtrudes the present into the past. One would approach the City silently, and solemnly, as if to avoid disturbing the rapt sorrows of this *Niobe*. One's sympathies are with the dead; whatever interrupts this train of feeling is harsh. Thus the distance thro the magnificent Porto del Populo shocks by it splendours, and one is called back, from conversing with the past, by the solicitations of present attractions.

The approach of Holy Week had already filled the City with a vast accession to the population. There were dense crowds in all the streets, and several hours were occupied in searching for accommodations. Evening drew on and we had the prospect of being all night in our carriages. There was no difficulty of getting something to eat at hundreds of shops but lodging seemed to be impossible. At length one of the numerous runners whom we had dispatched to search, returned and told us, that unfurnished rooms might be obtained in the Square of the Column of Trajan. Hither we drove and found a desolate sort of Palace with sixteen unfurnished rooms, which we might take at a hundred and fifty francs a week, and (that) we must take it for at least one week. By the time we had walked thro the house there was a crowd of menials, lacqueys, and all sorts of persons tending services and begging to be employed. We selected a half a dozen for our immediate necessities. One said he knew an upholsterer in the immediate neighborhood where we could hire furniture, another that he was a servant in a restaurant next door, and so on as to every possible demand a traveller might have. Fabre organized a numerous Commissariat, put each one upon his special department, and promised that by 9 o'clock he would have us comfortable. One of these employees turned out to be a fellow who said he had some property in our palace. He was constituted Major-Domo and things seeming to be got in trim, with a glint of sunshine yet on the top of the Column, Govan and I with a guide took our course for the Pantheon, that we might see if we could not find our way hence to the Capitol without a guide and that we actually effected; so just as twilight fell we stood upon the steps of the Capitol. In Rome more conspicuously than in any other place in the world, one need not expect to find any thing that has not been thoroughly pried into nor to experience any emotions which have not been described in prose or poetry. His would be a very strange idiosyncrasy, that would have different thoughts or impressions which have not been experienced by thousands before. There is no standpoint from which Rome can be looked at so peculiar as to be exclusive or particular. Every man who beholds it will soon find that he may be classed in a species. The most general division of class of observers is that into Protestants and Catholics. These two look upon Rome, not only with different, but with opposite and contradictory views. The one sees in every thing the consummation and perfection of a noble hierarchical system fraught with whatever is glorious in Religion and admirable in piety. The other, the Protestant, sees nothing but a degraded and creaking superstition depressing the human soul and body into vice and crime, with so deep a degredation that men are transformed to such an extent as not to perceive their foul disfigurement, but boast themselves more comely than before and are content to roll with pleasure in a sensual sty. This was the aspect in which things were presented to my Protestant eye. My Catholic companions saw in the City the triumphant manifestations of a great and well organized apostolic religion—Munificent foundations of Church.

A people sedulous of acts of religion slay the habitual presence of an active principle in the heart. No one failed to pull off his hat as a Cardinal drove by, or to bow his head as he passed an image of the Virgin. His sentiment of religion was impressed when he beheld the pocket handkerchief of Saint Veronica and his admiration exalted as he saw his devout fellow mortals prostrate themselves before a splinter of the true cross. A nice young lady said to me, "I am shocked to find in my own bosom a want of active sympathy in the devotions of these pious people. I ought to join in their prostrations. I am getting as bad as a Protestant by associating with you. I hope my confessor will prescribe a sufficient penance." Next to the divisions of Protestants and Catholics is that of those who live in the past and those who live in the present. The former and of the strangers they are the most numerous, enquire for nor see any thing in the City but history and tradition. The latter busy themselves about the state of Society, the state of private morals, public economy and civil polity, etc, etc. I soon found that I was thoroughly of the Protestant faction. My bosom was filled with sorrow, disgust, and horror, at the detestible superstition which had superseded the Church religion, and I saw or thought I saw the slime of the serpent everywhere, and the foul influences of his venom.

In 24 hours our palace Antonio was made comfortable by a profusion of furniture of all sorts, hired at what seemed to us a very small cost. Amongst other hired articles was a shew case of antiques for our drawing room—a piano for Mrs. Brown, and a flute for Govan. We took our meals at the shops. We hired a carriage, and added three servants to our regular establishment. Thus in the *Palace Antonio* we lived somewhat *"au grand."* Everything was amazingly cheap, the carriage at a dollar a day, each servant at 20 cents, they boarding themselves.

Of the objects which struck me most at first sight was first the Coliseum, a noble wreck in ruinous perfection. As a *ruin* I suppose the first in the world.

St. Peter's at first sight was short of my imagination; the emotion it excited was not so strong as I had expected. From day to day it grew until it became tremendous and oppressive.

The *Apollo Belvedere* and the Alps and the falls of Niagara are the only three things I have met in life whose actual presence transcended the imagination of them, and of the three, I am inclined to think that the Apollo most stunned and overwhelmed me. I was awed and rapt and my soul seemed to be expanded with a perception of the Perfect.

In Rome the things which struck me most forcibly were these and in this order—first the monuments of Antiquity, 2nd, the Specimens of Art, ancient, medieval and modern—3d, the strange preponderance in the population of priests, prostitutes, and beggars—these constituted the populace—and a most striking circumstance was profusion of water, foaming and splashing in magnificent fountains, and thence running in rivulets thro all quarters of the City. The first great object of Art and as I suppose the highest in the world is the *Apollo Belvidere,* the next perhaps, the Church of St. Peter's, which grows upon the imagination by successive visits much beyond the first impression until it oppresses and overwhelms one. In its conception, its execution, and its appointments I suppose it has no equal in the world in Ancient or modern times.—In the same way of all the ruins of the world I suppose the Coliseum is the most magnificent.—In the same rank of art with the Apollo is the *Transfiguration* by Raphael; that is each in its department [is] unique and unapproachable. *The Transfiguration* filled my heart with rapture and with a sort of adoration. I visited it very frequently and always arranged my dress for the visit as if I was going into some august Presence, which it was not fit that I should be in during my life. It seemed to me that such a transcendent monument of art ought not to be in a place of religious worship. One's heart could not rise into a pure devotion in the presence of such an attraction to the aesthetic and such sensuous qualities of our nature. The devotions mixed up with such emotions could not escape a sensuous admixture, and thus it is that the religion of the Roman Catholic Church has become supersaturated with sentiments of art, the admiration of which easily combines with adoration and evokes idolatry. Amidst one's devotions, the taste should not be offended, but on the other hand should not be so strongly appealed to, as to make it predominate, or to have a disturbing influence. The true medium is somewhere between the affected plainness approaching vulgarity of the Presbyterians, and the gorgeous profusion of ornamentation in the Roman Catholic Church. Of all things the most difficult in life is to fix the just mean wherein truth resides. Indeed altars at which a Christian congregation bends should not in my judgment be decorated with any objects of art. They distract rather than elevate the mind. The emotions are cognate but not identical. Even devotional services in churches should not be so artistically fine as to elicit artistical appreciations. Devotion implies and involves abstraction from the outer world—and an effort to attain however rarely successful should always be made. The ideal conception of our Saviour is always impaired by his sensible representation in Art, tho it be the art of Raphael or Da Vinci. The most exquisite manifestations of matter are still material and spoil the spirituality of thought. One experiences this effect on subjects of much less moment and excellence than those of religion. I have always regretted that I saw Hamlet or Falstaff represented even by the finest actors. When I now read the plays I see Kemble[90] or McCready,[91] and regret my ideal—obliterated by these actors.

While I was in Rome there were many eminent improvisators. The exhibitions of their art, tho admirable, did not fill me with the wonder expressed by others. My own experience from a very early age, that of 14 or 15, had taught me that extemporary utterance was not so difficult as is generally imagined, and implies no very peculiar intellectual endowments. Perhaps the only natural qualification necessary for it, is a capacity of utterance depending upon the organization of the vocal organs, their sensitiveness, their susceptibility to the impressions of thought, so that they respond promptly to the mental impressions. The rapidity of thought is so great as almost to exclude the idea of progress and inception. It is almost instantaneous. The rapidity of thought therefore is not as soon arrived at, and if the extemporary speaker or the improvisator is successful according to the delicacy of his vocal organs, with both thought always runs ahead of utterance and selects but does not create the materials. In both cases I am inclined to believe, is the faculty of an excited and rapid emotion, which from the whole mass of former impressions recollects what is proper for the occasion in hand, and instantly combines them into suitable arrangement. The materials must previously have existed in the mind,—they may have been slightly organized, or nearly obliterated,—but warmed by the excitement of extemporary speaking they spring out like sympathetic licks before the fire and the memory reads them. Now in the construction of all languages and perhaps in all human thought, there is a cadence and rhythm, which a nice ear and a flexible voice naturally catches and words to express this melody rise up and present themselves, or are recalled and pressed into service, by a rapid memory. In the writing of poety this rhythm is slowly and labouriously sought for and attained, altho many people lisp in numbers for the numbers come. The Italian improvisator has to deal with a language of infinite flexibility, which in ordinary conversation has a rhythmical intonation, most musical, and from the multiplication of vocalic terminations gives great facility to voices. Several of the performers exhibited great skill and when they became warm a most liquid stream of seeming passion was uttered and in such equable cadences that the accompaniment on the piano was in perfect accord. Doubtless the imagination caught up by the strain attributed both more perfect melody and harmony than was actually made and so the speaker when he has caught the sympathies of his auditors is apt to have beauties attributed to him which a cooler judgment would not perceive and it not infrequently happens that a speech perfectly reported in its sapiens verbis is declared to be different from what one had heard delivered.

But I wander from Rome. Let me return to our palace Antonia. Our mode of life was excessively laborious. The four and twenty hours were not sufficient for all the demands upon them. Bodily strength was exhausted and curiosity surfeited. It became necessary for us to arrange the programme for the next day's sight seeing and that we should proceed economically both as to space and time. Such arrangements were made in consult with experienced *Cicerones*. Our palatine domestic economy was somewhat of the strangest. We hired a large suite of servants at the head of whom was a sort of Major-Domo, in fact a factotum—his name was Peter and he was a Jew, whereupon we dubbed him Jew Peter. He was a man of intelligence and address, industrious, plausible and wonderfully au-fait, to all those little transactions of which we had occasion. He said that he had been in good circumstances, but by the unfaithfulness of subalterns had been reduced to indigence and now lived precariously upon temporary expedients except that he was the one third owner of the palace we had hired, and had also an interest in the furniture, which he said had belonged to him in his more prosperous days. He claimed kin with several apparently prosperous shop keepers about our residence —he made all of our bargains, disbursed all our expenses, and in short had our entire confidence. At length my man Fabre communicated to me mysteriously that he suspected Jew Peter to be an agent of the police and city, upon us, that he was not in fact a Jew, but went to confession in a neighbouring chapel and that all he said about the loss of property, was with very many other things he told us fiction. Upon revealing the case to Mr. Tarloucci our banker, he sent one of his clerks to investigate it. The result was that Jew Peter was no Jew but had been a servant for several years in the household of a church dignitary which he had quit without any imputation on his character, when his master went to Naples. Sending for a police officer, Jew Peter was arraigned before him, soon confessed that he had assumed a fictitious character, said that he had done it for a frolic and because Fabre had boasted that no man could impose upon him. He protested that he had been a faithful servant, asked the examination of his accounts which he produced, and they seemed to us to be correct. He declared that he had saved us from being cheated a thousand times and that he had been a vigilant and economical servant. "I appeal to you gentlemen," said he, "if I have not." We thought that he had and continued him in our service to Fabre's no little disgust. Peter had made in the course of the investigation some broad insinuations against Fabre, which we then suspected and afterwards knew to be well founded. Fabre reported that he had sold his carriage for 200 francs, and it turned out that he had received 330 for it. Our contract with [him] was that he should board himself, and it afterwards turned out that in his various bargains he had managed to get his own support, which he confessed that he had imposed upon those with whom we dealt, as the price which he exacted for his food bill in bringing customers.

The ceremonies of Holy Week and especially those of Good Friday and Easter, are in the highest style of scenic representation, holy and awful in the eyes of Catholics, theatrical and sometimes ludicrous to those of Protestants. That they have attained an artistic perfection is obviously true. The sentiments and the habits of the whole population from generation to generation, are trained to such exhibitions, and then too the physical condition of the city, is adapted to such scenic effects. No expenditure however lavish, no preparation however elaborate in any other city could achieve such results, as no expense or labour could have created such a church as that of St. Peter's out of Rome. The acting and the scenery was perfect, from the (—?) posse [?] down to the lamp business [?] and the scenery is the whole city of Rome. The night of the illumination of St. Angels was over clouded and therefore enhanced the effect. The benediction at St. Peter's was attended by more than forty thousand people, of all nations, tongues and costumes. The Pope, Pius VII,[92] was a feeble old man, and very much exhausted by the ceremonies at the high altar. In the eagerness of my curiosity I had lingered standing near the door at which the Pope was borne out. I was the only person standing and as the Pope was borne past me in his litter he raised up his tired left hand with the assistance of his right, and as his hand passed my head, pronounced a benediction. I instantly bent instinctively to my knees, and remained until the litter passed on. The venerable old man had a most divine and benevolent expression of countenance, with a touch of sadness and wearisomness. We had not got notice until an hour before the assemblying in the church that it was indispensably necessary to go there in full dress, that is don tailed coat and knee breeches. The last we were unprovided for, so we cut off our pantaloons at the knees, and stitched ribbands to them. This with my black pantaloons did not excite remarks, but as we stood in the crowd a company of English dandiers espied Govan's *pantaloons* and said loud enough for us to hear, "Dick, twiz that fellow's breeches." Govan, leaning forward, said, "If I catch you out of this church I will twiz your coat for you." Whether by accident or design a man from behind in uniform stepped between them, at the moment.

In Rome we made no acquaintances. We were at one crowded entertainment at the banker's Torlucci where I remarked that the only refreshment offered was ices and toothpicks on a waiter. At the end of eight weeks with a feeling that we had not examined any appreciable portion of the objects of interest and not without some petulance that notwithstanding exhausting efforts, we left so much unseen—but nothing not written in the Guide books,—we took the road one bright April morning to Albino, in the direction of Naples.

PART II*

From Albino we enjoyed a view of Ostia which in the clear light of an Italian spring morning was wholly visible. The air of the mountain was particularly agreeable after several hot days we had had in Rome, and was very refreshing to me whose health had been impaired for sometime. The quiet day therefore at Albino was altogether delightful,—and with renewed spirits we journeyed over the fine roads to Trasimeno, the ancient Auxus, a village situated on the margin of the Mediterranean. Upon a narrow beach below it and a high precipitous cliff, right fronting the piazza of our inn, discussing the probable elevation of the Cliff, Brown and I after the Virginia mode agreed to bet that I should go to a chapel on the top of it, and return in 15 minutes. He thought it double the distance that I estimated it, and he wagered our expenses from Rome to Naples that I could not make it in that time. I relied upon my familiarity in climbing rocks and mountains from childhood and was very confident of success. I was to make the ascent without a guide and to be allowed two minutes to breathe at a little inn which

* Editor's note: This is Preston's division.

seemed to be about half way up. The people of the village and some English travellers assembled in the piazza to witness the decision of the bet. Throwing off my coat, I essayed the Cliff successfully, made the Inn half way up in five minutes, and the shouts from below announced my victory, but when my two minutes and a half of rest had elapsed Mr. Brown called upon me to proceed. I found myself still panting and entirely exhausted so that I not only could not go on but had to call for a couple of guides to help me back. I gave up the bet and solaced my failure by the fact, which was too true, that I had been debilitated by my indisposition in Rome, for the consequences of my over-exertion under such circumstances, was a debility and depression the whole time of my visit to Naples. As to the bet I afterwards won it off by a bet with Mr. Brown that he could not upon two readings by me of an hundred lines from Homer's Iliad repeat them without more than two promptings. He required four promptings, Mrs. Brown being judge and holding the book in her hand. Brown looked grave and said it was the effect of approaching age, for that 20 years before he had won a bet upon repeating as many lines upon one reading. Mr. Brown was a joyous tempered and most accomplished man—beginning to pass middle life. It was a subject of much discussion and banter between us whether his age of 52 or mine of 20 was most fit for foreign travel—a question that I have never been able to resolve satisfactorily in my own mind. Just before Mr. Brown's death, the conversation happening to turn upon our old dispute, he said—"You were right, for you may have fifty years of the enjoyment of those pleasant memories. I can but have less than 20." In a few weeks he died of the apoplexy of which so many of our blood have perished. When I last saw him he had a list of 72 of our ancestors and collaterals who had perished in that way,—and he said to me, "You will go in the same way." From Trasimeno we went to breakfast at Nola di Gaeta. Breakfast was spread on a fine truss in an orange orchard, the table under the branches of an orange tree, hanging full of oranges of the last year's growth, whence we plucked and eat them. The fruit which has thus hung thro a whole season acquires additional sweetness the second year and was of much higher flavour than any I had ever tasted. Our seats were near and in full view of the sea, the Mediterraneum, whose very name is a history and a romance.

The Campagna Felix as we passed thro it was very beautiful but not so much so as when we repassed some weeks after in all its summer glory.

At Naples when we arrived at our hotel on the water, we were greeted by a congratulatory poetical address, by a poet. For its adaptation to us it was only necessary to insert variances in blanks left for that purpose in the manuscript. The poet pronounced it with a most oratorical declamation, and the portion of it for Mrs. Brown, with an operatic impressment that roused some confusion in the lady. Ten Pauls was suggested by Fabre as the quoddam honorarium of the Laureate, but Mrs. Brown thought it due to the particular elegance of that part of the poem which was hers peculiarly to add five Pauls, and we bought besides several copies of the fancifully adorned little book. It was perhaps owing in part to our liberality on this occasion that after dinner we were attended by a band of music in further celebration of our arrival, which struck up in our honour God Save the King. We found it hard to persuade the musicians that that was not our national tune, for altho they promptly and knowingly assented that we were not English, they insisted that it was the same thing, and that God Save the King must be our national anthem. Govan took his flute and played Yankee Doodle, as our tune, they looked somewhat blank and incredulous but in a few minutes made a plausible approximation to it. The next morning they came with the music scored, and played it, I think, better than I ever heard it before or since. We gave them a bit of gold, and they went off making the public walk resound with Yankee Doodle to the great amazement of the passersby to whom such a tune was a great novelty.

We rummaged Naples and its surroundings with great assiduity. One would be ashamed to attempt to say with what emotions. The politeness of the old banker Falconet, and of our consul Mr. Hawent [?] gave a personal and social interest to our sojourn,—besides some incidents in the nature of adventures.—Our trip to Mount Vesuvius was an amusing one. The old mountain was making some fine sightly exhibitions to us and occasionally thro the day puffing up smoke and throwing out stones so that a close inspection was attended with some little uneasiness as one ascended the side or stood upon the edge of the crater. Mrs. Brown, who was not without hardihood and curiosity, determined that she would go through the whole adventure with us. A portion of the long and toilsome ascent could be effected by riding, for which purpose donkeys were kept at the Cave. The gentlemen were easily accommodated, but there was no such thing as a woman's saddle in Italy. Mrs. Brown revolted with horror from the idea of riding man fashion. We could not obtain or contrive a palanquin. As necessity is the mother of invention we at length adjusted a chair to the back of the donkey with numerous straps and bonds round the body, neck, and tail of the patient animal, whose characteristic patience was most exemplary, and strapping Mrs. Brown too not a little with various cross plies she was at length crumpled up into a sort of sitting position. She was a good deal *au bon point*. Seeing a smile on my countenance she said, "Sir, if you laugh at me,—when we get to the Crater, I will push you over." There were four guides or attendants detailed for Mrs. Brown and her donkey, a little black shaggy beast very knowing and strong. One guide stood at each side to prevent the lady from falling backwards or forward, one led the donkey and one pushed him, when the ascent was beyond his strength. Thus we got on to the hermitage half way up, there refreshing ourselves with a bottle or two of pure Lacrima Chianti made from a vineyard on the spot. We got off our donkeys and essayed the ascent, on the rough surface of the cold lava, yet retaining some little warmth. Cords were put round our bodies and held by a guide to assist us, very stout active fellows; two of them, drew up Mrs. Brown's anchor. There was a broad strap of lathe at her back over which the cord passed. She had, I must say, a ludicrous appearance. When we got near the summit there were puffs of smoke and a slight shower of pumice issuing out of the crater. We crept along holding by the crags of lava, to get a peep over the edge into the depths of the abyss. In the interior deep down in it, the rocks were tumbling about like boiling water, with flashes of flame, and puffs of smoke; around us was a storm of wind, loaded with ashes and sulphur. Mrs. Brown in spite of remonstrances declared she would go as far as those who went furthest and see as much as those who saw most. So she was dragged up to the edge and peeped down, while the wind blew a hurricane over her. When we came to adjust ourselves for the descent, it was ascertained to our dismay that Mrs. Brown's gaiter boots had been left at the hermitage, she having nothing on her feet, but a pair of low shoes. The descent is not by the lava but through the pumice, that lies like shelled corn, and one goes plunging along the steep ascent, sinking over the knees or up to the waist. Govan and I ran down through it, leaping 15 or 20 feet at a leap and soon attained the bottom. In the meantime came on Mrs. Brown now held back by the two guides, the cord being removed. She came plunging along, knee deep in the pumice, having lost her shoes, and torn her stockings, her dress in the most tumultuary disarray, her bonnet hanging on her back, her frigette flying at random, the sweat streaming down her face, mixed with ashes, sulphur, and rouge. Throwing my cloak over her, I helped to get her into the hermitage. She said to me, "You are too much distressed to laugh at your kinswoman now,—but it will be a joke to you forever," and so indeed it has been for forty years, and Preston years from now, may read this and smile at the ludicrous condition of the willful lady who would look into the crater of Vesuvius. The lady's exhibition of fortitude and good temper was most exemplary, but I must say they gave way somewhat when after she was readjusted, the maid brought the forgotten gaiters, with an apology for not having sent them by the guide in the bundle. She threw the gaiters in the woman's face with upbraidings—In after years laughing with Mrs. Brown at the adventure I always omitted the finale of the gaiters.

Although Vesuvius was in a good deal of agitation during our stay at Naples, there was no eruption sufficiently violent or continued to require the liquifaction of the blood of St. Januarius, nor had we the pleasure of seeing the performance of any miracle whatever while we were in Italy. The miracle making functions of the Church were somewhat in abeyance while poor Pius the VII was dragged about through Europe by Bonaparte,[93] so that those who had a fancy for such exhibitions were disappointed during his reign. Certain pictures and statues, however, kept a sort of provincial miracle making for the vulgar—but even these declined to exhibit before Protestants until the dispensations of the holy court of Treves renewed the good old times of faith and showed a sufficient reaction to authorize the Dogma of the Immaculate Conception.

I was greatly struck with the stalwart proportion and muscular development of the Lazzeroni, and as much with a certain swagger and effrontery, resembling that of the finer mulattos of the Southern States. They did not seem to be inclined to offend or to submit to offence. The energetic reign I was told of Murat,[94] had in some sort reformed their morals and being much employed by him as soldiers and as labourers, on the public works, they had imbibed a feeling of maintaining themselves otherwise than on charity or by stealing, debasing conditions. They have always been a fierce and sometimes a courageous population. They have been out of the reach either above or below of the most deleterious influences of the Church, and thus have in some degree escaped some vices—such as cowardice, treachery and lying.

One day our party made an excursion to the excavations of Portici. Having fixed the day after for our departure from Naples, our passports were en règle, and the horses ordered for the morning. The intervening day was assigned to Portici, and it was as glorious a one as if no party had been contemplated. Portici is, I think, 16 miles from Naples. The day was spent amidst the strange excavations, and so far spent that when we mounted to retreat some extra speed was required to get back to the city by dark. A few Pauls secured the concurrence of the drivers and we moved at a quick pace until at the little town of St. John near the royal palace of Herculaneum we found our progress obtruded by a dense crowd in the street, it being a fête day. We got along through the mass, very staidly and with difficulty, in a slow walk, the people being unwilling to be disturbed in their enjoyments by the presence of the carriages. As we worked our way at this snail's pace we were surprised by the clatter of hoofs and wheels behind us, and the crowd falling back on each side made way for an open carriage with two men in uniform or livery seated in it and drawn by two fine horses. The carriage was drawn briskly along side of us, one of the men crying, "Make way." The crowd could not fall back fast enough nor could we drive on; thus the passing carriage had its wheels locked into ours and both stood still—both carriages were open barouches, and those occupying them stood in a few feet of each other. He in the opposing carriage snatched the whip of his driver, and began to belabour ours. Govan retaliated in kind, at which the man in uniform aimed some blows at Govan—Amidst the shouting of the populace at this spectacle, Govan who was as bold as he was strong, leaped at the opponent, dragged him out of the carriage on the pavement, and when I got to the scene they were upon the ground, Govan uppermost, the assailant with his face on the pavement, and kicking and struggling violently. I planted my foot upon the back of his head, and pressed his face upon the pavement, with some force, the mob the while vociferating "Well done." When I removed my foot he leapt up with a stiletto, which in the meantime he had drawn, and made at Govan with it. Govan stepping back from the aimed blow gave me time to run up behind and catch the fellow round both arms and drag him down upon the pavement with so quick a jerk that with a sudden slump in his fall the stiletto fell from his hand. There was an immense cry through the crowd of "a stiletto a stiletto," it being a highly criminal offense to have one in possession. While we were on the spot of the rencontre with my foot upon the prostrate man, a file of eight soldiers fully armed rushed through and surrounded us. The fellow getting up, the soldiers presented arms to him, and then for the first time we perceived that we had been dealing with an officer. The mob was clamorous that we had done right, and that he had got no more than he deserved,—and so we declared and spluttered in all the Italian we could muster. The head man of the file of soldiers, seeing the difficulty of our speech said to me in French, "Doubtless you may be right, but it is a bad affair, and you must go with us to the office of the police nearby"—and we were marched off accordingly. As we went I saw our coachman standing up in the carriage,—making a sort of harrangue how badly we had been treated, how patient we had been, and that if Govan had not been as daring as Hercules the huge blow given him by the officer would have knocked him out of the carriage.

The large room into which we were carried was on the second storey. It was fenced off at one end by an iron railing, and a large window opened upon an iron balcony that hung over the street. The village posse with some slight insignia of office in his button hole, took his seat at a desk and on either side of him a secretary with pens and paper. There was a great hubbub in the hall. Many at the same moment talked vociferously and pressed upon the posse to hear their account of the transaction. As length order was enforced, the hall was cleared by the soldiers of the mob, and the soldiers standing inside of the door railing with us—there were no other persons near, tho the crowd was in ear shot. The posse in a polite tone asked me to make a declaration of the conversation. I told him that I had not enough Italian to do so in that language,—but that I would do so in French if he would permit me. He consulted a moment with his secretaries, and "There is a Frenchman in the guards—and I will swear him as interpreter." It was done so and with great deliberation and with the utmost possible exactness, I stated the whole transaction, the interpreter writing it down in French and translating it to the secretaries who wrote it in Italian. When I got through the posse said, "I think the declaration is true, for I was in the street, and saw a good deal of the affair and it has been correctly stated. I must however examine a witness on some points." The interpreter was called, the same man who had spoken to me in French in the street. He circumstantially confirmed my declaration and the case wore a fair aspect. Night was closing in and as they brought lights I heard upon the stairs and saw in the crowd round the balustrade a considerable commotion. With the lamps entered a man in a uniform like that of our antagonist and with a consequential bustle took his seat by the posse, who rose to salute him. They entered upon an earnest conversation *sotto voce*. In the meantime the Interpreter whom I had begun to regard as a firm and efficient friend took his seat between Govan and me and we decided that the newcomer was a household officer of the Palace of Herculaneum, who had come to take jurisdiction of the case as having happened within the palatine jurisdiction and not within that of St. John. The conversation between the two officials, each asserting his jurisdiction, grew warm, each party urging his claim to us with earnestness. It soon appeared that the affray was exactly upon the line of the two jurisdictions,—part on each side, and this complicated the question with real difficulty—Mutual vehemence was manifested. Our sympathies were with the stout posse of St. John's, for it was apparent that the sympathies of the newcomer were with his fellow menial of the palace whom we had beaten. The two secretaries wrote with animated assiduity and seemed to second every thing uttered by the disputants. The household official ever and anon spoke with emphasis and an air of authority, but our St. John's posse maintained his jurisdiction with firmness and dignity and at length said that the police precinct was his,—to which the soldiers and our interpreter manifested acquiescence and that he would take the responsibility of trying us. Upon this the interpreter suggested a compromise, that he should be permitted to assist in the trial. In difficult cases none but the stoutest can resist the proposition of compromise however obviously fatal. Our St. John's posse yielded and agreed that the case should be opened, and that the adjunct might ask questions. The interpreter whispered me that I should say we were English officers and claimed the protection of English authorities, and "there will be an end of it." "But," I said, "we are not English." "Pshaw, say so,"—but he later acceded that we had best send up to Naples for Mr. Hawent. It was now past 10 o'clock, and going to the balcony there sat our coachmen on the box, having never moved. I threw a note to him and striking his horses he exclaimed, "I will be at the consular office in no time."

The first question propounded by the palatine was, "What countrymen are you?" The interpreter whispered, "Say English." I answered, "We are Americans"—not without some emotion of annoyance, prompted by the strangeness and difficulty of our position. He read over the Italian of my declaration, and said, "This you swear to." "No Sir, I will not swear in Italian, I dont know it well enough." "You must swear it or go to jail!" "I will not swear." The St. John's posse said, "*I* have received the declaration, there's an end of it." A doctor was called in who declared that we had beaten the man until his life was in danger, but we had only seen the patient standing in the street,—his face was bloody and his lip swollen. He declared to the doctor that he had struck our driver and Mr. Govan because we would not get out of the way when he was hastening to the palace, and that Mr. Govan's blows were much harder than his. The most extravagant lies were deferred to. Thro the Interpreter I kept up a pretty active cross examination, and thus maintained the integrity of the case. There was great dispute as to who had drawn the stiletto. The man swore that he had seen Govan draw it,—but it turned out that the fellow had not been there, and that the stiletto was the property of the household officer. (The office was that of purveyor for the palace). The secretaries wrote on the whole time and covered an immense quantity of paper. In one of the pauses of the trial we were permitted to go on the balcony. It was a sweet moonlight night. We were in a good deal of anxiety. Govan said to me, "Do you remember that man we saw in prison yesterday who had been there for thirty years until the offience charged upon him was forgotten?" While these thoughts were passing through our minds, we heard the rumbling of wheels coming from the direction of Naples. The carriages drew up and stopped. As we resumed our seats there was a hustle and we heard foot steps on the stairs. The consul entered in full feather in his regimentals and a huge sword by his side. We shook hands cordially. The judges saluted him respectfully. He said, "I have come to demand these my countrymen, in the name of my Country the United States of America. Here is my commission under the great seal as Consul general to all the Neapolitan dominions." The palatine was struck with awe, having an instinctive deference to one with a sword and uniform. The other judge said, "These gentlemen are in the hands of the civil authorities of St. John's." "Not so," said the palatine and the controversy was renewed. Mr. Hawent said, "I have nothing to do with the question of jurisdiction. I will take the gentlemen, and pledge my official honor that they shall be prosecuted tomorrow at 12 o'clock at [the office of the] chief of police, in Naples, where your question of jurisdiction— and the whole case may be inquired into." "Sign a paper," said the St. John's judge, "to that effect and you may take them." We joined in the pledge and were borne off in triumph by the consul. At my request the interpreter promised to attend. Mr. Brown whose constitutional timidity was very great, had driven straight at the beginning of the hubbub, on to Naples, and at day light the next morning availed himself of the already signed passports to Rome and was off. He had the kindness to wait for us at Rome for three weeks. *Mrs. Brown*, he said had been very much frightened.

The next day we with the Consul and the interpreter, were punctually at the office of the Chief of Police. At the end of three hours the officer took up the huge bundle of papers in our case, turned them over leisurely, and then said, "Attend here at this hour next Monday, under the guarantee of the Consul. I will take these papers home with me and let you know what I will do"—and bowing he unceremoniously withdrew. The consul exclaimed as he went out, "I will call at your office." "You need not," said the official, "Send your lawyer." We forthwith employed one recommended to us by the interpreter. A Signore Viconi was therefore introduced to us whose business seemed to be that of attorney or a man of affairs—not to look into the law of the case or to manage a judicial investigation but to solicit the Judge and to teaze him into an examination of the case. Signore Viconi was a middle aged grave looking gentleman of solemn aspect and slow movement, yet he repaired speedily and actively between his clients and the posse—Consul Hawent was greatly interested for us, but said it was a serious business and required time and management. Monday came; our lawyer presented a most voluminous memorial, as long, as unintelligible as a common law plea, with as many

involutions of phrase and superfluity of verbiage, with
the addition beyond the English law follies, of considerable
rhetorical flourish. The judge looked as
grave as did Sir Roger de Coverley's bull when he was
turned out upon the parish cows. He intimated that
perhaps the case ought to go before a higher tribunal
and took another [?] Hawent began to think that it
was like to be a very tedious affair,—and we to think it
might be an affair of years. We learned thro the Judge
that it had been the subject of conversation amongst the
palace menials and may have reached the royal ears.
Hawent regretted his want of Diplomatic authority at
the court—he being but consul. The Americans stood
very ill with the authorities. There was an unsettled
claim for Spoliations against the late government of
Murat, and Pinkney[95] with his secretary being on their
way to the court of Russia had been directed to go by
Naples and urge it strongly upon the bankrupt government.
These gentlemen, Pinkney and King, being entirely
ignorant of French or Italian, sent in a voluminous
communication, heard no more of it. Being so
bamboozled by spies, servants and officials that they did
not know at length whether they were in Naples or
Algiers, they fled, leaving Hawent to receive the answer
to their communication if it ever came. My servant
Fabre, who had been King's servant, and Hawent gave
me a most ludicrous account of the complications.
Hawent on his own account and as agent of Oliver of
Baltimore was a large claimant against the Spoliationers.
Just after Pinkney's and King's departure,
Commodore Barney with our fleet dropped suddenly

into the port of Naples—and in violation of law, brought with him more vessels than are permitted to enter. A good deal of sensation and indeed consternation was occasioned—and additional suspicions were excited when upon a formal annunciation of the breach of law of which the commodore avowed himself ignorant he would not withdraw his fleet until he had victualled it. While he lay in harbour some of his junior officers ashore got into a row—fired upon and repelled the police, wounding some of them. These circumstances produced an irritation against the Americans and complicated our case. It became the subject of conversation in the presence of the King,[96] who hinted that these lawless Americans perhaps intended an insult to officers of the Palace, and said it should be seriously considered of. The Marquis Circello, the minister of foreign affairs, who had been Ambassador to England, granted me a formal interview, told me of these things and seeing that the affair was a pure accident, and sprung from the misconduct of a rude menial, hinted in conclusion that it might be as well to run away if we could effect it, for that the King was a passionate man, and sometimes did things hastily—that if we could escape from the city no very vigorous pursuit should be made of us. This was a gloomy prospect. The weather was growing hot, and the demands upon our purse were exhausting. Hawent was of our most intimate council and the Interpreter an ardent retainer of the Murat régime and hater and contemnor of the actual government. We were apparently unrestrained in our excursions in the city but we soon found that there was always in sight of us a policeman who we did not doubt was a spy watching us. A plan suggested by Hawent was that we should get a harbour boat, row down to Ischia, and wait the chance of an English or American vessel passing. There were then many American vessels cruising near Naples. The interpreter was sent out to look for a suitable boat, and boatman. He found a one legged English boatman, who with a boy managed a light boat, who for ten francs a day agreed to row us to Ischia and be at our service as long as we chose. He was enjoined secrecy, and that we might know each other, we arranged that we should see him stealthily at his boat landing, and that he should know us by our giving him a lot of English money. We walked along the bank and seeing our wooden-legged friend sitting in his boat with an unmistakable English air, we called him to us and asking him if he could distinguish us by our looks from his own countrymen, he said, "Hardly, but I should take you for him across the water." I handed him an English crown piece and looking at it he said, "Aye, aye, Sir, I am ready," and with a knowing wink pocketed the money. We determined that two days afterwards we should essay our escape. The next day about 12 o'clock the Marquis Circello sent for me and said, "The King in a fit of impatience to be off a hunting this fine morning, when I suggested your case, said, 'Let the American canaille go to the devil.' Let me say so on your passport and go at once." He wrote a few words at the bottom of the passport, and said, "Go." Never was an order obeyed with more alacrity. By the time we had taken a lunch, the carriages with four horses were at the door, and we leapt in, flying like birds from a cage. It was a quarter past 4 o'clock. Handing in the passport to the officer at the border, he looked at the endorsement and touching his hat, said, "It is my duty to detain you." I showed him the writing at the bottom; he said, "Motto; hence it gives demands," and scribbled down his name.

The evening ride to Capua thro the Campagna Felix, was perfectly exquisite—the air soft and fragrant, the vines in full leaf trailed from one mulberry tree to another, and the peasants in their picturesque costumes bearing on their heads large baskets of mulberry leaves for the silk worms. The atmosphere was all fragrance and music and the solemn light of a sun descending upon soft and fertile landscapes to which the world can afford no parallel. Still we were not without some little sense of danger as we were in the domains of his Neapolitan Majesty, and our passport had to be viséed at Capua. The officer however only looked at the Naples signature and we passed thro Hannibal's ill starred quarters in the dusk not exposing ourselves to its seductive boundaries. Between Capua and Fondi the road is more infested than elsewhere by banditti, especially near the latter place. As we went South there were the road gallows on which hung the bodies of recently hung rogues, and there were many crosses by the wayside showing where bodies had been buried. It was proposed to us to accept the guard of a file of soldiers, but it was suggested that such an exhibition of care might excite the idea of having valuable treasure, which would attract the bandits and the soldiers would be sure to run from fear or on account of complicity with the robbers. It was indeed said that the soldiers were really bandits or members of Bandit families in the neighborhood. A few days before we passed, an English family had been robbed—the lady being compelled to lie down in the road in front of the carriage wheels until the trunks were searched and the linings of the carriage cut to pieces in which were found 158 napoleons in gold. Many such stories were circulated and almost daily robberies were taking place. Brown and his wife had been in great terror as we went down. As we returned Govan and I consoled ourselves that we should not be much worse off in the hands of the banditti than in those of the Neapolitan police and drove on nearly all night.

About sunrise we were in Fondi, the Capital of the banditti. It was said to be a sure nest of robbers. The postilions would not agree to stop for breakfast, and said that we could get none if we stopped. From a shop we bought a bottle of oil and a loaf of brown bread which I found very palatable and thus learned that oil was a most excellent substitute for butter, a piece of information that has served me in good stead in after life. We breathed freer after having passed the boundaries of Naples and gradually lost the feeling of flight—but we plied our journey without stop and with such speed as could be made over the fine roads of the Pontine Marches, as fine a road as I have ever seen except that from Mantua to Tindaro. As we drove on rapidly there was a house near the road, from which smoke and flames were bursting, and we heard the shrieks of a woman from the inside. We hastened to it and saw amidst the dense smoke a frantic woman, tossing her hands and screaming. She was instantly extricated and then began screaming, "My child—my child!" Govan muffled his cloak around his head, and plunging into the burning house brought out a child of two years old. His clothes were a good deal singed and his hands burnt. Stepping down to the canal to wash his hands, he found there a fisherman watching his cork in a state of the most placid serenity. He said it was not his child and why should he trouble himself about it. Govan advanced towards him to knock him into the canal but I said, "Remember St. John's." Our postilions had manifested an equal indifference—not coming near the house or the woman. They said, "It is not our business." On the whole route thro the Pontine Marches, the postilions and all the inn keepers of the places where we stopped to change horses were sallow and feeble, seeming to be in very ill health. Many indeed were prostrated with the marsh fever at this early season (May).

As we drove on to Rome the lamps were lighting. We had made the 170 miles in about 26 hours. It was with great delight that I found myself again in Rome. Every man has a sort of citizenship there, for it is the capital of the human race, and then the government of the old Pope, his mythical hierarchy is so exempt from caprice, so regulated by a quiet traditional policy that no one under it is exposed to the rude petulance of impertinent officials or exactions of aught, but the solemn farce of an everlasting routine. I felt comfortable and disposed to take mine ease. The next morning I bathed, dressed and went to make my respects to the *Apollo* and the *Transfiguration.* We took lodgings at the hotel de Espagna. Brown a little ashamed of the precipitency with which he had left us in the lurch, laid it upon Mrs. Brown, who promptly said that she had wished to stay and see us through. This putting the leaving of us on the basis of the timidity of Mrs. Brown is another proof that woman besides being a solace in times of quiet may be a protection in time of danger. The pretext was accepted as a valid excuse and Mr. Brown's mortification at his own conduct, made us the more willing to reestablish our "entente cordiale."

A week was spent busily and pleasantly in Rome—and we took the road for the Alps and Gaul. We struck straight for Florence—of all places that I have ever seen, the most beautiful and attractive. Whatever nature could do in her most lavish moods she has done for it, and then it is decorated with all that prodigality of art which wealth and taste for centuries could bestow upon it. Nature has bestowed upon its landscape, the Arno, Fiesole and the Val d'Arno, art has given it the churches and palaces of Michael Angelo and Raphael, Tasso and Dante have conferred upon it the glorious associations of poetry, and the magnificent *Medici* family concentrated in it whatever is beautiful or noble in the productions of the pencil or the chisel—the *Madonna della Seggiola* and the Venus di Medici and all this is enwrapt and enblazoned in a climate the most enchanting and glorious. The surrounding blue covered mountain sides of Albano, Fiesole, uttering the names of Gallileo and Milton, rears its top into the clouds, and the pellucid Arno flows gently thro the city. Surely there is not upon the face of the earth a spot comparable to it, one that so fills at once the soul and the senses with scenes of and sentiments of beauty. Naples with its bay and its volcano is grander—Rome with its solemn memories more awful but neither has that aggregation of beauty which gratifies so intimately all the aesthetic faculties of human nature. To breathe the air was a luxury, to open one's eyes was to see a glory, and if you closed them what memories flowed in upon the soul. Science and Literature and Philosophy—and courage and fortitude. I said to myself a thousand times, "If exile from my native land should be my destiny may it be in *Florence*!" and now at the [end] of forty years, with a body broken by disease and a heart by misfortune, my memory grows warm as it hovers over that glorious city. It had been a frequent dream of my life while I enjoyed the sweet companionship of that lady[97] whose death has wrapt the remnant of my life in gloom, that we should go together to Florence and there live and love our closing days. She was a fit person to be amongst and to grace such scenery, to be associated with such art and such nature. I shall never see her or Florence again. They are kindred objects in my memory.

It was "au courant" with the agreeabilities of Florence [that in] the suite of rooms we had at the Scheidor hotel were a music room, baths and a fine conservatory with a garden attached, all for ten francs a day, our meals being furnished from a neighboring *restaurateur* as we might order.

The Venus did not strike me so agreeably as I had expected—beautiful doubtless—"beautiful exceedingly." My raptures were restrained and modified by those circumstances which seemed to be evolved from a subsequent analysis of my emotions. The statue is too small—below nature. I think she does not seem to be fully grown. The average height of woman is now and I suppose in all ages has been above five feet. Venus is below. The attitude is inexpressive. The countenance has a bad expression—it is not that of purity and trust. It is not that of a virtuous woman. The nudity of the figure is not pleasant. With female beauty we always associate the idea of drapery, and of colour too. In the male figure we can readily dispense with these accessories of drapery and colours. The *majesty* of the male figures may exclude or reject these things. *Majesty* may supply the place. We can well conceive a grand naked man when wild in woods the native savage ran—but a naked woman is positively unpleasant. I doubt whether her configuration is so conformable to the lines of beauty as that of the male. The majestic is hid when the man is enveloped in a blanket or a buffalo robe and revealed when the covering is thrown off, as I have seen amongst the Indians, and marble or bronze may fitly represent it, but beauty can't stand the garish and vulgar light. Modesty is an essential element of female beauty, at least it is to the civilized and Christian mind. Woman is picturesque but not statuesque. Upon the whole the Venus is too *petite*. I take it that Eve was five feet, an inch, perhaps two, high—that before the fall at least she had a modest look, which Venus has not, and thus that as the ideal of female loveliness it is defective. The ancients had not that ideal. It is of Christian origin. In the gallery of the portraits of eminent painters each painted by himself, I was proud to see that of our countrymen was Gilbert Stuart, one occupying with all the characteristics of a fine painting a very conspicuous place amongst its illustrious compeers, vindicating by its own merit its right to be here in Florence amongst the illustrious artists deposited by the Italian taste here in this pantheon.

The lower classes of Florence and the peasantry of Tuscany were better looking, seemed more contented and happy than I had seen elsewhere. The eye was offended by fewer priests, prostitutes, and paupers than in any Italian town. The three classes bear a natural relation to each other, they flourish under the same form of religion—and civil polity. The reigning Duke[98] is said to be a good man and a wise ruler, his manners are free and genial. He is seen frequently at places of public resort, attended with so little ceremony, that one passes him without recognizing him. He values himself upon his horsemanship, keeps a stud of fine English horses, and is proud to show his skill in riding by dashing amongst English or American horsemen—his own countrymen offering no competition with him in the art of riding. Indeed an Italian on horseback is a ludicrous object and the ladies astraddle upon their high trotting horses are horrible.

From Florence to Bologna we took a conveyance by vettura, that is we hired an equipage, consisting of two carriages with three stout mules in each—the driver being the owner, and the contract with him being for the whole job stipulated the various lines and stages. It was of some consequence to us to put ourselves in the charge of a good tempered and faithful contractor, for we were of course very dependent upon him for our comfort. We were to be at no charge except horses, meals and lodging. Our conductor, the person who owned and had charge of the carriage and who was the driver of our, that is of Govan's and my carriage, we going ahead, was a young fellow of about two and twenty, stout, handsome and of very gay temper and manners. His father came with him to see us start, and while he gave his son many charges as to his good conduct and discretion, he entreated us to have a kindly care of the boy for the old man's and the mother's sake. He said that he was a good son and a good boy, but that this was only the second time that he had been in the exercise of the family vocation put at the head of an expedition of such *illustrious* a party. Our contract was drawn and vouched by a notary public—the father being a joint obligar with the son. We paid half the passage money in advance (forty dollars). Our handsome vetturino was full of spirits and confidence. He wore a gay cap with a silver tassel in [it], sky blue round about coat, a red jacket and other articles of dress conformable, he wore a broad, heavy cue tied with many knots, a brand new cloak, and blazing new jack boots. With unrestrained pride he showed us his fine mules—well made, fat, and gentle, with a most affectionate understanding between them and their master.

One young mule was a special pet upon whose merits he descanted with praise and to which while they were yet being greased he from time to time gave a bit of brown bread from his pocket. Her eyes followed him in the crowd expecting the gratuity. All things were ready, the father at the coach window was adjusting the interior comforts, and turning to me he said, "Have you a St. Anthony?" Supposing that he meant a coin I handed him two pauls. He stepped into a shop and returned with a little leaden figure of St. Anthony, presenting it to me, and also one to his son, saying that he commended us to his patron saint—to him of Padua—enjoining upon us that as we passed thro that city we should stop and pay our devotions at the equestrian statue of which I had a leaden model in my hat. Faithful to the injunctions of the old man when we got to Padua we made our respects to the huge awkward St. Anthony, mounted on a great horse rushing along in a sweeping pace, as awkward a motion for a great groom as ever was seen upon a high road. Whether it was that my taste was offended by the great big ugly statue so as to disturb my veneration or from whatever cause, also for the inefficacy of invocations, images and patron saints, we had not proceeded but one stage beyond Padua, when the sorrel mauve mule tripped as we trotted down a gentle declivity, and falling down prostrate skinned her shins and her side, lying helpless from the shock. Her station in the team was the post of honour, that of near horse behind saddle horse, as the wagoners term it. Joachimo was pitched off into the dusty road, and as we all applied our strength to back the carriage off the fallen mule and to assist her to rise, Joachimo's pity and rage were at once ludicrous and terrible. I never heard such volubility of swearing. The Italian language is most copious, next to the Greek, in oaths and cursing, and the pale rage of the Italian is frightful. Joachimo wept over Nina, threw his fine cap into the dirt and trampled it under foot, tore the ribbons from his cue,—broke out against St. Anthony with the most violent imprecations, denounced him as a most damnable and hypocritical saint, not fit to be trusted with any thing better than a Jack Ass, said he was a scoundrel, a liar and a thief, swore that Nina was worth twice as much as the great cast horse the saint rode which he hoped would fall and break his damned saintly neck. Mr. Brown treasured in his memory this torrent of abjurations and often repeated it as a high sample of Italian improvisation. Poor Nina stood trembling and subdued amidst the sympathizing group around her. At length Joachimo's rage began to subside into the softer mood of pity; he cut off a large bit of bread and presented it, but Nina made no sign of taking it. She did not even smell at it, or move her nose as her master rubbed the bread against it. An hour's repose seemed to restore her much, and she was manifestly refreshed by an half a quart of aqua vita which Joachimo very anxiously administered from a black bottle we happened to have in the carriage. Fortunately the rest of the stage was down hill, and proceeding slowly, Nina was so much recovered that a night's rest seemed to have quite relieved her the next morning. Joachimo too rose in much better spirits, professed shame and penitence for his assault upon the saint but put him on good behaviour. In the course of the morning's drive however the unfortunate Nina cast a shoe, and as the vetturino began to boil with rage we hinted that perhaps his rough treatment of St. Anthony had something to do with it—and that as we had a good deal of journeying yet to do, he had best be particular. Joachimo took the hint and as we had six miles to the next smithy, he took a strip blanket and wrapped it round under the hoof, securing it on the pastern, so that the mare got on clumsily but without pain.

At Bologna, now a forsaken and dilapidated old town, I saw with the greatest admiration Raphael's picture of St. Cecilia, a production but little short of his finest Madonnas. With somewhat ashamed emotions I ascended through the long continuous gallery to the top of a high hill to see the celebrated portrait of the Virgin Mother painted by St. Luke, and miraculously brought from Palestine by angels to Bologna. The sacred relic is on the altar of a church built for its reception, and is enclosed amidst blazing jewels in a frame of gold. The artistic merit of the portrait is not high, it looks more like a charcoal sketch by a boy, and if the correct likeness of the original, she could not have been so beautiful as she has been represented to be in the treasured paintings of Raphael. The doors which enclose the holy portrait for the profane gaze of curious eyes, were opened by a priest with many gesticulations and much muttering of prayers. We were required to kneel and gaze. As we left the church, giving to the showman his accustomed fee, I said, "As a specimen of art I dont think it is very high." He said, "You English are Protestants."

From Bologna we turned west to visit Modena and Parma, being willing to see the late Empress[99] who held her little court at Parma. We saw her at the theatre. We sat within ten feet of her and had a view of her for an hour. She was pale, haggard and almost scrawny, affected very little state. There were but six or eight attendants amongst whom was the Austrian[100] who was said to have taken Napoleon's place in her bed. Whether they had children I did not learn nor have I learned since. The theatre was a dusky place. The Duchess sent a person in waiting to invite the English gentlemen, as she took us to be, to come into the boxes. We explained that we were Americans and bowed out of the theatre. I could but think of the lines of Byron

> "If she still loves thee hoard *that* gem
> Tis worth thy vanished diadem."

The expression of the lady's countenance seemed to me to he hard and homely, and sad. It excited no sympathy but rather the opposite feelings. We returned in the direction of Venice, crossing the Po at Ferrara, a most desolate village. In the palace of the Estes was a flock of goats, and we traversed a long street in front of it without seeing a single human being. The town had been lately inundated by a crevasse in the Po. We crossed the river ascending a steep bank to the boat— and were drawn across by the strength of an impetuous current, the boat being attached by a cord to the opposite bank, with the side presented to the current, at such an angle as to impel it across.

Going down the Brenta we stopped for breakfast on the bank of the river. There was a boy at the window dragging with a small net for frogs. We ordered our breakfast of them; the boy charged us for 72 frogs. They were very small and only the hind quarters were served up. They were exceedingly delicate and savoury.

Venice—that silent city—seems rising up from the water. It is filled with historic recollections but not with histories that address themselves to the heart and imagination like those of antiquity. Who cares for the Doges, or their wars with the Turks?—who feels to the Lion of St. Mark as towards a Roman Eagle, or towards the Maltese Cross, or to the Lebanon? In its amphibean existence, it has not belonged properly to the land or the water, it does not belong to antiquity or to the Middle ages, or to Modern times. The place St. Mark is doubtless magnificent, with its winged lion and horses of Lysippus. Its gondolas look mysterious and have a touch of romance upon them—But I saw nothing in Venice that so filled my imagination as the *Rialto* where merchants most did congregate,—one touch of Shakespeare has sanctified it as a stroke of lightning hallowed the object it struck. The place *looked* and I thought felt damp—objects of art were not frequent, at least of the very highest order. No smiling prospects, no exciting rages, no picturesque objects but the black monotonous gondola very calmly slipping or rather stealing about. Lord Byron[101] was living in the city in that state of ostentatious profligacy horrible to every body but to the English nobility to whose impurities his vices gave a countenance while his transcendent genius seemed to shed a lustre upon their caste. Strange that so exalted genius should be found combined with such transcendent vices. In his heart there was no one virtue, in his conduct no one rule of morals which he did not violate—no praiseworthy sentiment of human nature that he did not outrage. The blessed sympathies of son, father, husband, citizen he outraged, and scorned, and all this was coupled with intellectual endowments of the very highest order. Attracted by their lustre I was inclined by a sort of horrid fascination to see the Monster and learned that on certain days of the week he admitted the visit of strangers. I felt the temptation but rejected it, and only saw him as he stood in his gondola, as mine rowed by him. The gondolier said, "That's Lord Byron," for all knew him as one of the lions of the city. We were near enough to see his figure but not to see his countenance, and that is all that I saw of Cain, Conrad, Manfred, and Don Juan; it is sad and painful to add to the list Childe Harold.

At Parma Mr. and Mrs. Brown left us to go straight to Milan and wait there for us while we made the run down to Venice and back. We agreed to dine with them at Milan on a day fixed. Leaving Venice we went to Mantua. We spent a day there with Vergil and the next we went to dine with our friends at Milan. To effect this we left Mantua at day dawn, as the drums were beating for the opening of the gates. We informed the postilion of our haste, for the interest of speed, gave him a double fee, and told him to let each postilion at the successive posts [know] of our rate of pay. The roads were perfectly straight and as level as the graveled walk of a nobleman's lawn—the horses in the finest plight. We changed every ten miles, and the changes, thanks to signals given on a bugle, were effected in two minutes. The new postilion would say, "Is the carriage strong? Will you risk it?" "Aye, aye," we replied, and he darted off at half, sometimes at full speed. No stage took us more than an hour. The distance to Milan was 37 leagues, and we drove through the porte-cochère as the dinner bell rang. We had put on our dinner dress as we came on, and walked in with the party, with a tranquil air as if we had just left our chamber. I had a certain consciousness of having made an achievement. There is no point of vanity more common in young men than to have made rapid rides. They brag at each other about it. We were manifestly enhanced in the estimation of some Englishmen at the table, for our trip implied two things that always go to the heart of an Englishman, namely bodily assurance and a lavish expenditure of money.

The great political importance of Milan and the many historical associations with it are scarcely thought of by the visitor in his eagerness to behold the Cathedral —the great glory of Gothic Architecture—for while York Minister and the Cathedral at Rouen are in many particulars fit rivals for it, the aspect of the French and English Cathedrals and indeed of Gothic architecture generally is gloomy and Egyptological. The colouring of them is sombre, the effects are brought out rather by shadows than by lights,—and where lights are admitted they are taught to counterfeit a gloom. They have the grave colour of all big things—of the Elephant, the Rhinoceros or the Lion. In England, in Germany, and at Rouen houses being built of a sombre coloured stone they are further embrowned by the climate. Here this wonderful structure is of white granite, of a glittering white, shining in the translucency of an Italian atmosphere—so as not to represent the gloom of a primeval forest, but rather the dazzling effect of a glacier, bright and cold. The infinite multiplicity of ornaments, the intricacy of the traceries, the interleaving of carvings and frettings look like frost work. The general effect is not *Gothic* but rather *Arabesque*—and there is an incongruity in the sentiment intended. The Gothic style of architecture belongs to a Northern climate, not to that of Italy. It belongs to a form of worship, modified amongst forests and by the stern and hard nature of rude peoples emerging from Druidical rites or from the notions of the Valhalla. In Italy lie discovered the tastes of a refined nation, the sentiments of a gay and gorgeous paganism,—obviously yet pervading and controlling the whole body and spirit of papal worship. York Minister is the type of one sort of worship, St. Peter's of the other. The Cathedral of Milan is not thoroughly of either. In its construction elaborately Gothic—by its material and the lights in which it is seen Italian.

In the neighborhood are quarries of beautiful white granite. Bonaparte had ordered a triumphal arch to be built in the city of it. Some of the columns lie unfinished, some half finished near one of the gates. When one contemplates the magnificence of the terrible conqueror and then sees in the streets the wicked panderers and the fierce hussars, who have come in his place one cannot but regret the change of master for this fair land. The Austrian domination is fierce and coarse, a hard despotism of unmitigated force—a mechanism inexorable in its action. The city was full of Austrian soldiers. I never met a file of them but with a feeling of indignation akin to vengeance. How must it have been with the Italians?

From Milan we visited the Lakes, very beautiful, differing from the Scotch lakes in this—that here in Italy you are always in view of some touch of art, some exquisite monument, some depiction of natural beauty by a stroke of art. You are never as in Scotland in the presence of primeval nature and nature where the Mighty Mother reveals her peerless charms. The elements of delight are thus somewhat different—perhaps the highest pleasure is in nature unordered, her charms are perhaps peerless. I do not decide. Maggiore and Como are surrounded by villas, the islands adorned by elaborate and elegant architecture, a monument or a hermitage on each point of rocks, and something illustrating each point of view. They are not destitute by any means of historical or poetic associations, but these are not so thickly or so touchingly clustered around them as at the Scotch Lakes, where tradition and song and ballad in the sweet minstrelsy of Scotland twine all over them like lichen over a rock and cover them up with verdure and tendrils and sweet little flowers and he the mighty Minstrel has from his own glorious success and glowing heart shed a light upon them more warm and soft, than ever has been bestowed upon Italian Lake and mountain scenery. In general the delight of natural scenery is enlivened by the perception that it is remote from and has been rarely invaded by men. The sensation becomes almost awful when one is impressed with the idea that the scene is beheld for the first time by a civilized eye, and the idea is novel and agreeable as it approaches this extreme. I have experienced it in the wide reachless prairies where the deer and wolf had not learned my human nature, and sometimes too I have approached it amongst the deepest recesses of the Alleghanies. The idea too presents itself amongst the most savage scenes of the Scotch highlands, or on the margin of its most lonely lakes. The feelings incident to such situations are marred by the presence of any trace of man or of the work of his hand, except from those springing from poetical associations. They spoil or mar nothing but enhance and glorify every thing. Poetry is a stronger or a softer light thro which we look at nature; it does not disturb but only shows her features.

It is with a sad and sorrowful feeling that one quits Italy, to take the Alps,—but they obtrude new images upon the mind, and the beauty of soft scenes which has had possession of the soul is superseded by the sublime and terrible, the toilsome ascent thro the snow and glaciers, to the summit of the *Simplon.* At the Hospice the mind puts off its Italian vestments and prepares for new adventures. I bought one of the huge snow dogs half grown, for thirty dollars, and called him Alp. I took a regular bill of sale for him from the friar of the convent, which I found necessary to exempt me from the charge expected to be made of having stolen him. Taking the northern declivity of the Alps my mind sprung to Paris, where besides its pertinent attractions, there was a sort of home attraction to Legaré, Petticolas, the DesPinardes, Stewart and other loved friends. Brown too had preceded us, for he and his wife declared that they would rather see the Place Vendôme than all the lakes of Italy or the world. Thus we came back to a circle of intimate friends, giving us a cordial reception.

NOTES

1. Mrs. Rion, wife of Colonel James H. Rion, distinguished South Carolina lawyer, whose son was named for Preston.
2. Francis Preston and Sarah Buchanan Campbell Preston.
3. Colonel William Preston. For an account of Preston's family—its origin in Great Britain and its history in America—see the sketches contributed to *Virginia Historical Portraiture* (published by the Virginia Historical Society, 1930), by Mr. Preston Davie, a kinsman of William C. Preston.
4. In his *Historical Sketches and Reminiscences of An Octogenarian*, Thomas L. Preston, brother of William C. Preston, quotes an article on William C. Preston, written by Virginia Preston Carrington, niece and adopted daughter of William C. Preston. The article appeared originally in *The Sunny South* (August 20, 1887).
5. Preston's only child, who died in young womanhood.
6. The salt works in Smythe County, Virginia, owned by the Preston family.
7. Now Washington and Lee University.
8. Founded in 1801.
9. In his *Biographical Sketches of the Bench and Bar*, J. B. O'Neall testifies to the oratorical abilities of young Preston: "I have heard him in college, at the Bar, in the State Legislature, and on many other occasions during his public life, and I confess, as to mere oratory I think he was, in college boyhood, as perfect a speaker as he was in after life. He afterwards acquired more knowledge, more powers of argumentation, but he never exceeded himself in his youthful display of eloquent declamation."
10. Hugh Swinton Legaré (1789-1843), orator and statesman. He became Attorney-General of the United States, and served for a time as Secretary of State.
11. George McDuffie (1788-1849) was Governor of South Carolina from 1834 to 1836, and later United States Senator.

12. Benjamin Watkins Leigh (1781-1849), distinguished Virginia jurist and politician.

13. Abel Parker Upshur (1790-1844), Virginia statesman and jurist. In 1841 he became Secretary of the Navy, and in 1843, Secretary of State.

14. Matthew Stephenson (1776-1834), Virginia statesman, noted for his liberal views.

15. A reference, no doubt, to Moses Hoge of Hanover Presbytery (1752-1820), an eloquent preacher. In 1806 he beçame President of Hampden-Sidney College.

16. Perhaps William Edward West (1788-1857), a famous artist, is referred to.

17. John Wickham (1763-1839), a distinguished lawyer from Long Island, who settled in Virginia in 1785. He was counsel for Aaron Burr in the latter's trial for treason against the United States government.

18. Henry Clay, who had been elected to Congress in 1811, was at this time Speaker of the House.

19. Langdon Cheves (1776-1857), eminent South Carolina jurist and politician. He distinguished himself as a member of Congress, succeeding Clay in 1814 as Speaker of the House. In 1816 he became a judge of the Superior Court of South Carolina.

20. In later years, from 1836-1842, Preston was Calhoun's colleague in the United States Senate.

21. William Jones Lowndes (1782-1822), a South Carolina statesman, for five terms a member of Congress. Clay had the highest respect for his abilities.

22. George M. Bibb (1772-1859), jurist and statesman. In 1844 he was appointed Secretary of the Treasury.

23. James Wilkinson (1757-1825) became Governor of Louisiana in 1805. In 1811 he was court-martialed on a charge of conspiring with Burr against the Government and with being in the pay of Spain. He was acquitted, owing, it is said, to lack of evidence, and in 1813 he was made a Major-General. He wrote *Memoirs of My Own Times.*

24. Charles Pinckney (1758-1824) and Charles Cotesworth Pinckney (1746-1825). The former was Minister to Spain and the latter, Minister to France.

25. William Branch Giles (1762-1830), Virginia politician. He represented Virginia in Congress and in the Senate, and in later years was elected Governor of his state.

26. William Harris Crawford (1772-1843) represented Georgia in the United States Senate and in 1816 became Secretary of the Treasury.

27. Richard Cutts (1771-1845), a Congressman from Maine, married Anna Payne, a sister of Dolly Madison.

28. Edward Coles (1786-1868), private secretary to President Madison from 1810-1816. In 1817 he was sent on a secret mission to Russia (Preston makes mention of this later) and in 1823 he became Governor of Illinois.

29. John Payne, brother of Dolly Madison.

30. John Payne Todd (1792-1851), Dolly Madison's son by her first marriage.

31. General Winfield Scott married Miss Mayo in 1817.

32. John Randolph of Roanoke (1773-1833), orator, statesman, and wit.

33. For additional information regarding Preston's visit to Washington, see the article on Preston in *The Land We Love* (August 1868).

34. William Wirt (1772-1834), distinguished jurist and statesman. He was Attorney-General from 1817-1829. He wrote a biography of Patrick Henry.

35. William Cabell Rives (1793-1868), statesman, diplomat, and author. Among his writings is *The History of the Life and Times of James Madison*. He was on intimate terms with Madison and had access to his manuscripts and papers.

36. A reference perhaps to *Thomas* Gillmer, who became Governor of Virginia in 1840.

37. In March, 1817.

38. Mrs. Bradish had been Washington Irving's landlady.

39. Luther Bradish (1783-1863), statesman and diplomat.

40. Gulian Crommelin Verplanck (1786-1870), politician, scholar, and essayist.

41. David Hosack (1769-1835), noted scientist and physician.

42. John Wakefield Francis (1789-1861), physician, editor, and biographer.

43. William James MacNeven (1763-1841), physician and professor in the College of Physicians and Surgeons. He was the first scientist to establish a chemical laboratory in New York.

44. Samuel Lathan Mitchill (1764-1831), the "Nestor of American Science."

45. Nathaniel Prime, head of the firm of Prime, Ward, and King, at that time the leading banking-house of New York.

46. Maurice John Braham (1774-1856), noted English singer.

47. Archibald Hamilton Rowan (1751-1834), United Irishman, and one of the victims in the State trials of 1794-1803. In his youth he spent a few months in South Carolina as Secretary to Lord Charles Montague and in later years resided again for a time in America.

48. The most famous speech of John Philpot Curran (1750-1817), the Irish politician and orator, was in defence of Hamilton Rowan.

49. The heroine of Lady Morgan's most popular novel. To her admirers Lady Morgan, née Sidney Owenson (1783?-1859), was known as "Glorvina."

50. Preston's interest in the Copyright was keen and deserves recognition. He interested his friend Washington Irving in the subject.

51. Charles Philips (1787?-1859) was famous for his pleading. He was a leader of the Old Bailey Bar.

52. James Maury, consul to Liverpool from 1789-1837.

53. A mistake. Irving, who was born in 1783, was Preston's senior by eleven years. For an account of the friendship between Irving and Preston see the article by Minnie Clare Yarborough—"Rambles With Washington Irving"—published in *The South Atlantic Quarterly* (October 1930).

54. Washington Allston (1779-1843), "the American Titian," was born in South Carolina.

55. Charles Robert Leslie (1794-1859), American genre painter, designed illustrations for the *Sketch Book* and for *Knickerbocker's History of New York*. He painted a portrait of Irving.

56. Gilbert Stuart Newton (1794-1835), an English artist. He painted portraits of Scott, Tom Moore, and Irving.

57. Irving's *Sketch Book* notes, which became the property of Yale University in 1926, were edited with a Critical Introduction by Professor Stanley T. Williams, and published in 1927 (New Haven).

58. Preston means *Pindar* Cockloft. If we accept Preston's testimony, Peter Irving, as well as William Irving, had a part in *Salmagundi*.

59. Peter Irving, who was born in 1771, died in 1838.

60. Louis Francois Roubillac (1695-1762), the famous French sculptor.

61. Both DeQuincey and Washington Irving allude in their writing to Lady Eleanor Butler.

62. An allusion to *Salmagundi*.

63. For Irving's account of this excursion, see *Tour In Scotland and Other Manuscript Notes by Washington Irving*, edited by Stanley T. Williams (New Haven, 1927).

63a. [*Preston's Note*] Govan, the college acquaintance thus resumed began an intimacy which continued thro life. He was the son of a proud lady in Orangeburg, [South Carolina] a man of hereditary wealth. He was a representative in Congress for many years from the Orangeburg district. He married an heiress in North Carolina, and upon some reverse of fortune moved to the West whither their mother sent his sons to my care while I was president of the South Carolina College. Govan was of an elegant and most athletic person, more studious of his physical accomplishments than of his mental. He took lessons in dancing, fencing, exercise of the fire lock and in boxing, and was quite *au fait* in each art. He was of so fine a temper that every body loved him.

64. Albert Gallatin (1786-1849), diplomat and public financier. He was Minister to France from 1816-1823.

64a. [*Preston's Note*] Mr. Warden was by birth an Irishman. He is represented somewhat *colour de vain* by Lady Morgan in her book on France, but he was in truth a most excellent gentleman of wide information and his book [*Statistical, Political, and Historical Account of the United States of America*] is full of valuable matter. On his card was engraved *ancien consul des États Unis,* which he continued to use to a decrepit old age. He had been rudely thrust out of office by H. Crawford [William H. Crawford, Georgia statesman, was appointed Minister to France in 1813], who was "dans son naturel" a coarse man.

65. David Bailie Warden (1778-1846), who was born in Ireland, came to America when he was very young. He was a graduate of the New York Medical College. In 1804 he was appointed Secretary of the Legation to General John Armstrong. He was later appointed Consul to Paris and held the office for forty years.

65a. [*Preston's Note*] At that time Senator in Congress from Louisiana, afterwards for many years [1823-1829] Ambassador to France. His mother was daughter of John Preston, my great grandfather. John Brown and his brother had also been senators from Kentucky. James was a lawyer at New Orleans where he made a very large fortune, [and] invested in a sugar plantation. He was a man of considerable talents, of uncommon accomplishments, and of great wit and brightness. It was a frequent subject of discussion between us which was the fittest age for foreign travel, his or mine, I being 20 and he fifty. His wife, a sister of Mr. Henry Clay's wife was an uninteresting and frivolous woman. Brown died in Philadelphia while I was in the Senate.

66. Preston's college friend. See note 10.

67. Jean Baptiste Isabey (1767-1855), noted French portrait painter, who painted the most illustrious persons of his time. His "Napoleon at Malmaison" is regarded as the best picture of the subject.

68. Francois Joseph Talma (1763-1826), distinguished French actor, who advocated realism in costume and scenery.

69. Catherine-Joseph Rafuin Duchesnoise (1777-1835), French tragedienne.

70. Anne Francois-Hippolyte Boutet Monvel Mars (1779-1847), a great French actress. She has been described as "incomparable in ingenue parts and equally charming as the coquette."

71. Arnold Scheffer (1796-1853), editor and political writer. He was a brother of the painter Ary Scheffer.

72. In a vituperative review of *France* in the *Quarterly Review* for August, 1817, John Wilson Croker accused Lady Morgan of ignorance, falsehood, and licentiousness.

73. *Les Liasons Dangereuses* and *Les Guerres des Dieux* by Parnay are the books referred to. See Croker's review.

74. Commenting on Lady Morgan's ignorance of the French tongue, Croker says: "She describes the cottages in Normandy as 'Deeply buried in their *Bouquets D'arbres,* or knots of fruit and forest trees,' p. 35.

"If it were not for Lady Morgan's own officious translation we should have thought *bouquet,* nosegay, a mere error of the press for *bosquet,* a grove or tuft of trees, etc."

75. Armand-Emmanuel du Plessis, Duc de Richelieu (1766-1822), well known diplomat and statesman.

76. Pierre Etienne Dumont (1759-1829) edited the works of the famous English jurist, Jeremy Bentham.

77. Carlo Andrea, Count Pozzo di Borgo (1766-1842), Russian diplomat. On the restoration of the Bourbons he became Ambassador at the Tuileries.

78. Pierre Simon, Marquis de Laplace (1749-1837), the distinguished mathematician and astronomer.

79. Dr. Thomas Cooper (1759-1840), educator and political philosopher. He served as President of the South Carolina College from 1821-1833. Preston was on intimate terms with him after his removal to Columbia, South Carolina, in 1822.

80. Nicholas, Prince Esterhazy de Galantha (1767-1833), noted Austrian diplomat.

81. In the year 1825.

82. Governor Richard I. Manning (1789-1836). As an aide-de-camp of Governor Manning, Preston received the title of Colonel.

82a. [*Preston's Note*] Stewart Newton, a nephew of Gilbert Stewart, the great American portrait painter, was a young artist of the highest promise. Died early (I believe). Leslie attained eminence in his art, and is now member of the Royal Society. Petticolas was also an artist friend and companion. Our lodgings were in the same suite of apartments. He was a perfect enthusiast in his art. Upon my return to Richmond he attained eminence as a portrait painter, and after years of ill health and hypochondria died in a Lunatic Asylum in Williamsburg. Next to that by Healy he painted the best portrait of me in my twenty fifth year, which is now in the possession of brother Thomas.

83. The statue by Roubillac. See page 39.

84. Emilie Bigottini (1785-1858), talented and popular French dancer.

85. Angelica Catalani (1780-1849), Italian soprano.

85a. [*Preston's Note*] *Washerwoman*.

86. Lady Mary Wortley Montagu (1689-1762), famous for her delightful letters.

87. For details of the fate which befell Horace Walpole's little black spaniel, see Gray's letter to his mother, written from Turin on November 7, 1739.

88. Victor Emmanuel I. Piedmont was restored to the house of Savoy after the Congress of Vienna in 1815.

89. Dr. Robert W. Gibbes, scientist and physician, who was born in Charleston in 1809, endeavored to establish a public museum of Natural History in Columbia, South Carolina. His collection was destroyed when his residence was burned in 1865 by Sherman's invading army.

90. Evidently Charles Kemble (1775-1854). John Philip Kemble had retired from the stage shortly before Preston's arrival in London.

91. William Charles Macready (1793-1873). Preston may have seen him act at Covent Garden in 1819.

92. Pope Pius VII (Luigi Bernaba Chiaramonti), born in 1740, became Pope in 1800. He died in 1823.

93. Pope Pius VII, made a prisoner in 1809, was taken first to Grenoble, then to Savona, and later to Fontainebleau, to await the return of Napoleon from Moscow. In 1814 he was liberated and the Papal States were returned to the Church.

94. In 1808 Joachim Murat (1771-1815) was appointed King of Naples by Napoleon.

95. William Pinkney (1764-1832) served from 1816-1818 as Minister Plenipotentiary to Russia and special Minister to Naples. He endeavored to secure indemnity for losses suf-

fered by American merchants during the Murat regime in 1809.

96. King Ferdinand. In 1815 when Murat sailed for France the Austrians entered Naples and restored Bourbon rule.

97. His wife, Louise Penelope Davis Preston, who died thirteen years before her husband. The Diary which she kept for a short time during her residence in Washington, when Preston was a Senator, contains some valuable references to Calhoun, Clay, and Webster. This brief journal, which is unpublished, is now the property of the University of South Carolina.

98. The grand duke Ferdinand III, who was reinstated in 1814, after the fall of Napoleon.

99. Marie Louise (1791-1847), the second wife of Napoleon. In 1816 she was granted the Duchies of Parma, Piacenza, and Guastalla.

100. Count von Neipperg, with whom Marie Louise lived before Napoleon's death. He became her morganatic husband and they had several children.

101. Lord Byron (1788-1824) was living at this time in the Palazzo Mocenigo on the Grand Canal.

CHRONOLOGY OF WILLIAM CAMPBELL PRESTON

1794. Born in Philadelphia, Pennsylvania, on December 24.
1808. Became a student at Washington College in Lexington, Virginia.
1809. Journeyed South for his health and entered the South Carolina College.
1812. Was graduated from the South Carolina College.
1816. Traveled to the western frontier.
1817-1819. Traveled abroad and studied at the University of Edinburgh.
1820. Was admitted to the Virginia bar.
1822. Married Miss Maria Coalter and settled in Columbia, South Carolina.
Entered upon distinguished legal career.
1828. Elected to the South Carolina Legislature.
1829. Death of his wife.
1830. Reëlected to Legislature.
Advocated Nullification.
1831. Married Miss Louise Penelope Davis.
1832. Elected for a third time to State Legislature.
Visited by Washington Irving.
1836. Elected to the United States Senate.
1836-1842. Made memorable speeches in the Senate on the Abolition Question, the Annexation of Texas, the French Spoliation Claims, and the Veto Power.
1842. Resigned his seat in the Senate, owing to unwillingness to act with Calhoun in the latter's support of Van Buren's policy.
1843. Delivered eulogy in Charleston, South Carolina, on Hugh S. Legaré.
1845. Became President of the South Carolina College.

1846. Received from Harvard the degree of LL.D.
1847. Death of his second wife.
1851. Resigned the presidency of the South Carolina College.
1851-1857. Served as trustee of the South Carolina College.
1858 [?]. Began to write his *Reminiscences*.
1859. Opposed Secession.
1860. Died in Columbia, South Carolina, on May 22.

INDEX

Addison, Joseph, 74
Allston, Washington, 36

Barney, Commodore, 103
Bentham, Jeremy, 58, 59
Bernard, John, 10
Bibb, George M., 6
Bigottini, Emilie, 67
Bonaparte, Napoleon, 54, 70, 94, 121
Bradish, Luther, 22
Bradish, Mrs., 22
Braham, John Maurice, 28
Brown, James, 53, 56, 57, 69, 72, 88, 89, 102, 107, 109, 115, 119, 124, 128
Brown, Mrs. James, 75, 80, 89, 90, 91, 92, 93, 102, 109, 119
Burke, Edmund, 31
Burns, Robert, 49
Butler, Miss, 40
Byrnes, Peter, 2
Byron, Lord, 117, 118, 119

Calhoun, John C., 6, 7
Campbell, Thomas, 35
Campbell, General William, 2
Carrington, Mrs. Eliza Preston, 2
Catalani, Angelica, 67
Cheves, Langdon, 6, 126
Clark, George Rogers, 15, 16, 55
Clay, Henry, 6
Coles, Edward, 8, 9, 28, 29
Coles, Miss Sally, 8, 9
Coles, Samuel, 66, 67
Constant de Rebecque, Henri Benjamin, 55
Cooper, Dr. Thomas, 59
Crawford, William Harris, 7
Croker, John Wilson, 56
Curran, John Philpot, 29, 30
Cutts, Richard, 8, 9

Davie, Preston, 125
Deas, Colonel, 62
Duchesnoise, Catherine-Joseph Rafuin, 54, 55, 64, 67
Dumont, Pierre Etienne, 57, 58, 59

Esterhazy de Galantha, Prince Nicholas, 60

Ferdinand, King, 104, 105
Ferdinand III, Grand Duke, 112
Fox, Charles James, 7
Francis, John Wakefield, 22

Gallatin, Albert, 51, 53, 57, 58, 59, 66
Gallatin, Mrs., 59, 60
Gibbes, Dr. Robert, 76
Giles, William Branch, 7
Gillmer, Thomas, 10, 127
Govan, 50, 54, 69, 74, 75, 78, 80, 91, 93, 96, 97, 98, 100, 101, 107, 108, 113
Gray, Thomas, 69, 130
Green, Professor Edwin L., IX

Henry, Patrick, 2
Hoge, Moses, 6
Hosack, David, 22

Irving, Peter, 36, 38, 43
Irving, Washington, 32, 33, 34, 35, 36, 48, 49
Isabey, Jean Baptiste, 53

Jackson, Andrew, 33
Jefferson, Thomas, 21, 32

Kemble, Charles, 82

Lafayette, Marquis de, 55, 61, 62
Laplace, Pierre Simon, Marquis de, 57

[137]

Legaré, Hugh Swinton, 6, 53, 54, 65, 124
Leigh, Benjamin Watkins, 6
Leslie, Charles Robert, 36, 63, 67, 127
Lowndes, William Jones, 6

Macready, William Charles, 82
McDuffie, George, 6, 125
MacNeven, William James, 22
Madison, Mrs. (Dolly), 6, 8, 9
Madison, James, 6, 7, 8
Manning, Governor Richard I., 61
Marie Louise, Empress, 117
Marshall, John, 8, 58
Mars, Anne Francois-Hippolyte Boutet Monvel, 55, 64, 67
Maury, James, 32, 33
Mayo, Miss, 8, 9
Mitchill, Samuel Latham, 22
Monroe, James, 21
Montague, Lady Mary, 69
Morgan, Lady, 29, 55, 127
Morgan, Sir Charles, 29
Murat, Joachim, 54, 95, 103, 104

Neipperg, Count von, 117
Newton, Gilbert Stuart, 36, 63, 67, 128

Payne, John, 8
Petticolas, 67, 68, 124
Philips, Charles, 30, 31
Pinckney, Charles, 7
Pinckney, Charles Cotesworth, 7
Pinkney, William, 103
Pius VII, Pope, 87, 94, 108
Ponsonby, Miss, 40
Pozzo di Borgo, Carl, Count Andrea, 57, 58
Preston, Francis, 125
Preston, Louise Penelope Davis, 110, 130
Preston, Sally, 2, 125
Preston, Sarah Buchanan Campbell, 125

Preston, Thomas, 125, 130
Preston, Col. William, 125
Prime, Nathaniel, 22

Randolph, John, 9
Raoul, Dr., 53
Richelieu, Armand-Emmanuel du Plessis, Duc de, 56
Rion, Mrs. James H., 125
Rion, Preston, IX, X, 94
Rives, William Cabell, 10
Roubillac, Louise Francois, 39
Rowan, Archibald, Hamilton, 29, 30

Scott, Sir Walter, 46, 47, 48, 49
Scott, General Winfield, 8
Scheffer, Arnold, 55, 61
Smollett, George Tobias, 49
St. Pierre, 56
Stephenson, Matthew, 6
Stuart, Gilbert, 112

Talma, Francois Joseph, 54, 55, 64, 67
Todd, John Payne, 8

Upshur, Abel Parker, 6

Verplanck, Gulian Crommelin, 22, 55
Victor Emmanuel I., 73

Walpole, Horace, 69, 70, 72
Warden, David Bailie, 53, 54, 56
Washington, George, 41, 58
Wayne, General Anthony, 3
Wellington, Duke of, 59
West, 6
Whaley, Hercules, 3, 5
Wickham, John, 6
Wilkinson, General James, 7
Williams, General David R., 62
Wirt, William, 10

Young, Lovick, 62

www.ingramcontent.com/pod-product-compliance
Lightning Source LLC
Chambersburg PA
CBHW030115010526
44116CB00005B/251